WHEN WOMEN DIVE

A FEMALE'S GUIDE TO BOTH DIVING AND SNORKELING

W9-BSD-931

BY ERIN O'NEILL AND ELLA JEAN MORGAN

Disclaimer

Diving is a potentially hazardous practice and if practiced incorrectly or with incomplete planning and procedures can expose a person to considerable risks including serious injury or death. It requires specialized training, equipment and experience. This book is not intended as a substitute for the above or for the diver to abandon common sense in pursuit of diving activities beyond his abilities. This book is intended as a source of information on various aspects of snorkeling and diving, not as a substitute for proper training and experience. For training in diving, contact a national certification agency. The reader is advised that all the elements of hazard and risk associated with scuba diving cannot be brought out within the scope of this text. The authors, publisher, and manufacturers presented in this book, are not liable for damage or injury including death which may result from scuba diving activities, with respect to information contained herein.

Book Design and Typography by Creative Input
Photography and illustrations by Morgan/O'Neill, except as noted
Cover design by Theresa Lambert
Cover photo by Morgan/O'Neill

First Printing 1992
Watersport Publishing, Inc., P.O. Box 83727, San Diego, CA 92138

Printed in the United States

International Standard Book Number
ISBN 0-922769-11-7

Library of Congress Catalog Card Number: 91-68417
O'Neill, Erin and Morgan, Ella Jean
When Women Dive
A Female's Guide to Both Snorkeling and Diving

WHEN WOMEN DIVE

A FEMALE'S GUIDE TO BOTH DIVING AND SNORKELING

BY ERIN O'NEILL AND ELLA JEAN MORGAN

Watersport Publishing, Inc.
Post Office Box 83727
San Diego, CA 92138

ACKNOWLEDGMENTS

In writing this book, we have experienced the tedium and fatigue known to all writers, but also the exhilaration of seeing this project grow and blossom. We are elated by the prospect of bringing a new outlook to women entranced by diving and who are struggling alone with its challenges.

This book has come about because of many people: Friends, relatives, diving students, dive buddies, and strangers. We thank you all. There are a few special people we recognize here because of the meaningful part which they played.

Bob Beck, *for his love, steadfast support and trust in us.*

Phyllis Villareal, *for her enthusiasm, for leading the way, and for generously sharing her knowledge.*

Kathleen Fisher, *for her designing, editing, typesetting, and high energy through out the doldrums, and for her friendship.*

Ken Loyst, *for his nurturing of these writers and for his encouragement and belief in the existence of this book.*

TABLE OF CONTENTS

Dedicated to excellence in all things.

CHAPTER ONE

A Brief History

"What's a lovely girl like you doing in such an abominable sport as this?" asked the prop-man. "Well, Mr. Blaine," I replied, "I'm here because I love what I'm doing. Aquatics is my life. I never get tired. At the end of the day, I am rested, refreshed from being in and out of the sea, and I really feel bathed and very clean. I'm very curious and I'm following my bliss. This is a very happy place to be."

Zale Parry

Almost half a century ago, the self-contained underwater breathing apparatus (scuba) was developed. It was immediately perceived as a useful military tool, and hence most of the early research and development was done by men with men and warfare in mind. Most of the testing was done by the military.

Scuba diving, however, was quickly discovered by other men who had recreation in mind, rather than war. They bought their diving gear from Army and Navy surplus stores, and thus began the sport of scuba diving.

In 1954, Los Angeles County in California began to train instructors in the techniques of teaching safe scuba diving. At first, diving courses were very short as the students came well prepared primarily from the skin diving (breath-hold diving) community. Skin diving was considered a very masculine sport, requiring great strength and courage which was automatically transferred to scuba diving.

It was a small step to take an accomplished skin diver and add the necessary knowledge to make him a scuba diver. Equipment was limited and there were few equipment oriented skills to learn. There were no submersible pressure gauges, reserve valves, buoyancy compensators, wetsuits, redundant second stages and all the other equipment that we use today, equipment that makes today's diving safer and more comfortable.

Photo by Donna Emmanuel

Divers come in all ages and both genders.

Even though the sport has traditionally been male oriented and male dominated, women need not feel that they are intruding in an area which belongs naturally or exclusively to men. From the inception of sport diving, women have played significant, pace-setting roles in the field of diving. In spite of several books and abundant articles on the subject, many divers of both sexes are unaware of this.

As more and more equipment has been added, making our sport easier to master, the sheer number of people scuba diving on a regular basis has risen dramatically. Every year the number of women entering the ranks of divers has increased. Because equipment is now being made specifically for women, we now have gear that does not need to be drastically altered to fit us. We can dive in wetsuits designed for us, in buoyancy compensators that fit, and in fins that come in more than one size. So, many things have changed.

Although entry-level dive instruction has certainly become much longer and more comprehensive since 1954, there are still essential details which cannot be covered in the scope of an entry-level class. This missing information is important to all divers, but particularly so to women, some of whom emerge from their training classes intimidated, frustrated or overwhelmed by the equipment or skills.

This is a sport in which a woman has to take her basic physiology, anatomy, emotions, common sense, future plans, medications, and personality into consideration. Mastering how these apply to the sport will make skin or scuba diving more enjoyable, far safer and much more comfortable.

Photo courtesy of Zale Parry Neuman

Zale Parry before riding a wet sub from the California coast to Catalina island in 1955.

CHAPTER TWO

Gateway to
Adventure

"Snorkeling has opened up a whole new world to us. It has kept us active and in contact with people who are doing interesting things."

Louise and George Hughes, ages 77 and 79
Piedmont, California

If you have never been underwater, you are missing a world of great beauty and peace. No matter what else is going on in your life, it ceases to exist the moment you drop beneath the surface. Many people feel safer underwater because there are no auto accidents, no street crimes, no rapes, no robberies, not even taxes! The stress of your everyday life immediately falls away as you become one with your new environment. You discover that time underwater passes very quickly. You will find yourself wanting to extend dives. Problems you had imagined prove to be untrue.

It doesn't take long to get comfortable underwater.

It's great fun to interact with sea animals.

In the underwater world, you are weightless as you float and glide among the beautiful reefs and the colorful fish. They seem curious and friendly; you feel welcome in their world. They seem to understand that you come in friendship.

There are few threatening or dangerous animals. Moray eels aren't terrifying creatures ready to strike. They are very shy, near-sighted animals who breathe through their mouths and are quite happy being left alone in their small homes. Octopuses are small, timid and retiring creatures who are terrified of divers. Sharks of the Hollywood variety are hard to find. You must search and search to perhaps find one as sharks mostly avoid divers.

Unlike a zoo, there are no fences between you and the interesting and intriguing creatures who inhabit the reef. You can get close to untamed critters, you can feed them by hand, you can observe their behavior in their natural habitat. This is truly a most glorious new world, and all you had to do was put a mask on your face and peer in.

13

If you are not quite ready to undergo full scuba diver training, consider learning to snorkel. From there you may progress to skin diving. The difference between the two is that snorkeling is limited to observing from the surface of the water and watching the ocean go by beneath you whereas in skin diving, you take a deep breath and dive down beneath the surface and become closer to the reef and its inhabitants. Snorkeling and skin diving can provide many hours of contentment and enjoyment. Even after many years of scuba diving, we continue to relish the opportunity to go snorkeling or skin diving. The skills you need to learn are simple and within the abilities of everyone. However, you should complete a formal class to ensure that you safely learn the techniques you need.

Good skin diving skills add to comfort in the water.

As you progress from a snorkeler to a skin diver and descend below the surface of the water, you need to learn about surface dives, equalizing the pressure in your ears, equipment, weighting, buoyancy systems, fin kicks, marine life and much more. The following chapters in this book will help you with this information. Much of this information applies equally to snorkelers, skin divers, and scuba divers.

Once you master being on the surface snorkeling and skin diving, you may find an increased interest in learning to scuba dive. If you choose to scuba dive, it is an easy step to go from skin diver to scuba diver as the skills you have learned skin diving are utilized for scuba diving also. However, if you don't want to scuba dive, you can still become a good snorkeler or skin diver and enjoy yourself immensely – don't feel pressured into scuba diving. As a good skin diver, you may even achieve a level of comfort missing in many scuba divers.

If still unsure but interested in scuba diving, you do not necessarily have to commit yourself to a full certification course. There are a couple of other options.

The first is a mini-course, or an introduction to diving. This program requires only a couple of hours. In this type of course, you use mask and fins and scuba to actually experience breathing underwater on scuba in a pool or other quiet water. This introduction to diving helps you decide on a future commitment as you will rapidly discover how you feel about being underwater.

A more complete experience is called a "resort course". It is designed for the person who merely wants to experience diving in the ocean, usually in a warm water locale, without undergoing a certification course. This course consists of an orientation to the elementary details you need to know to stay safe and a dive under the watchful eye of an instructor. These courses involve only a few divers at a time in order to provide individual attention to each diver. This type of experience may be just the ticket for you if you only want to dive this one time, or if you want to try the sport before you invest the time, effort and money in a full certification course. It is the first step in diving and has been taken by thousands of people around the world.

If you have decided it is time for you to "get wet" and complete a scuba diver training and certification course, here are some hints about scuba courses.

A scuba certification course is designed to give you the skills and knowledge to allow you to dive safely. Since you need to be well trained, your instructor and the course you choose are of vital importance to you. You are not simply embarking on a two-hour lesson on the ski slope. There are many hours to be spent in the classroom learning how being underwater affects you, and in the water learning and practicing the skills you need to dive safely when the course is over.

The ultimate goal of everyone entering a scuba class is to receive a certification card (C-card). This card will certify that you have successfully completed your diver training course. You will need it to purchase or rent equipment, take dive trips and fill your tank with air. It's your license to dive.

While there is only one place to get a driver's license, there are quite a few associations or agencies that issue diver certification cards. These certifying agencies have differing opinions about how much a person needs to know and how well they need to perform in order to qualify as a fully certified diver. These organizations train and certify instructors who in turn trains you. Each differs in what it requires of its instructors. So, all scuba classes are not created equal, and your training may be conducted by instructors vastly differing in experience, ca-

Scuba class is not only informative but it is also fun.

pabilities and training. You want to get the best training from the best instructor.

Table 2.1 lists the major certifying agencies and some examples of what they require for certification.

You spend generally between twenty-five and fifty hours in your class, depending on which course you select. What's the difference between these long and short courses? It is the overall course content. Some associations feel that a basic grounding in the use of the equipment, some medical information, some of the elementary skills, exposure to shallow water, etc., is enough for an entry-level course. Because of this limited exposure they recommend that you enter more advanced training after completing the entry-level course. However, a problem can occur when a certified diver from a short course attempts to do some forms of diving without the recommended advanced courses. If you choose a short course, pay heed to the recommendations to follow up your entry-level course with the additional training. This is vitally important for your safety.

Other associations consider it necessary to more fully school you from the beginning going beyond the minimum levels. These associations believe it is necessary for you to have additional knowledge of skin diving skills, oceanography, marine life, rescues, navigation, deeper water, etc., because they want you to be more capable right from the beginning.

Training also varies somewhat by region. For example, Los Angeles County certification courses require that you make your class dives in the ocean. Since Los Angeles County is on the ocean, this makes perfect sense. In other areas, students who receive their training in landlocked areas make their dives in a variety of bodies of water. Some courses even allow you to do the preparatory classroom and pool work in your local area and the actual open water diving in a more appropriate location such as a diving resort. This would certainly appeal to the person in Chicago learning to dive in January, wouldn't it?

Minimum Entry-Level Standards of American Diver Training Organizations

Table 2.1

Agency	Inception Date	Minimum Hours	Min. Days	Min. Dives	Diving Days
LA Co.	1955	27 (9 lecture) (9 pool) (9 ocean)	5	5	2
YMCA	1959	32 + Ocean (14 lecture) (18 pool)	n/a	5	2
NAUI	1960	28 (17 water)	5	5	2
NASDS	1962	None	n/a	5	2
NASE	1983	26	4	5	2
PADI	1966	None	n/a	4	2
SSI	1971	None	n/a	5	2
IDEA	1978	32	n/a	6	3
PDIC	1979	None	n/a	5	2
MDEA	1984	40	n/a	6	3

Minimum training standards indicate the varying philosophies of how much is necessary to include in diver training; obviously, there are differences. There are some divers who want to get through the certification process as quickly as possible, while others are more concerned with the substance of their course. Some associations place emphasis on the comprehensive content of their initial certification course, while others delegate some of the same material to subsequent courses. Note: There are other training organizations outside of the U.S. that are not included in this table.

(In the table, "n/a" means the agency does not specify a minimum number of days needed to become certified.)

When shopping for training, it pays to do some research before deciding which course to take.

Ask:

1. Which training agency issues your certification cards? How many overall hours are required? How are the hours allocated to classroom, pool, and open-water?

2. How many open-water dives are required? Four? Five? Six?

3. How is a dive defined? Agencies define a dive in various ways; time, entry into and exit from the water, the amount of air breathed underwater, depth, etc.

4. How many days of open-water training? The course with the most days offers the greatest advantage to you.

5. What topics are covered in the classroom? Is an instructor always present?

6. What water skills are taught? Some courses do not include skills like skin diving, buddy breathing, and emergency swimming ascents.

7. Where will the open-water dives be held? Will you be introduced to different locations? Will you have any boat dives?

8. What will be the activities during the dives? Will you learn skills like underwater compass navigation and rescue work?

9. How many students will there be in your class? All agencies have a maximum number of students to instructor ratio for open-water training. If your class size exceeds eight, the group will be divided, or other instructors must accompany your class.

10. What is the price of the course, and what does that price include? Do you have to pay extra for texts, dive tables, and other learning materials? Will your equipment be included, or do you have to purchase or rent? Is the cost of any boat dives included?

So, you have a lot of questions to ask and decisions to make when you begin to inquire about training in your area. Don't be mislead by the title of a course; you will be best served by a course that includes all the skills and information you particularly need regardless of what the course is called (see Chapters 4 through 7). Whether you choose to acquire this knowledge within the framework of one longer course or two or more shorter courses is up to you. *Remember, you will appreciate the quality of your training much longer than you will remember the price of the course.*

Enroll in the best class you can find.

A course which delivers less than the minimum training standards required by the respective agency would certainly not be approved of by that agency. Any violation of an agency's minimum standards should immediately be reported to the agency. The agency would then take appropriate action.

In addition to the course content, it is important that you have good rapport with your instructor. This is a critical course for you and you are going to be spending a lot of time with this person. Go to the trouble

Pool practice during class prepares you for the ocean.

of meeting the instructor before making a commitment. This is vital. There are all kinds of instructors. However, the instructor you want will be happy to meet you and answer your questions about the course to your satisfaction.

A word of caution, many divers exaggerate their experiences. Stories of incredible, life threatening happenings during training are often greatly embellished. If these accounts cause you to dread some exercise or aspect of your training, discuss it with your instructor. You will find that your fears are groundless.

Traditionally, scuba classes are offered at retail dive stores. Their business is to train people in the safe way to use the equipment they sell. Many colleges and universities also offer dive instruction, and professional teaching facilities independent of the stores are also available around the country.

At most facilities you are required to purchase your own "personal" gear. This usually consists of a mask, snorkel and fins, and often booties and gloves. Monetarily, this adds up quickly. Since you've been required to purchase before you've had any experience with dive equipment, get help from the course instructor and the professional sales people in the store. Ask for a commitment from the store for an exchange if your choices prove less than you'd hoped.

An entry level dive course prepares you for a limited range of diving situations. Any conditions differing from those in which you are trained require special consideration. Diving in a fresh water lake does not qualify you for venturing into the ocean. Booking a spot on a boat going to a deep wreck immediately after certification may not be your cup of tea if the deepest dive you made during your class was 35 feet (10 meters). If your entry-level course was short and sweet, you may need to take the next one or two classes before making these more involved dives. You need this additional training to become the best diver you can be. The more competent you are, the more you will enjoy your diving.

CHAPTER THREE

Your Body
In Action

"Diving has given me so much more confidence. Maybe it has something to do with being a woman, but there is such a feeling of accomplishment in mastering something that's physically challenging — something that you doubted you could accomplish."

Nancy Latham
Siapan, Micronesia

You thought completing your certification course in scuba diving was going to be enough, and that your C-card insured your place among sport divers. Although you are right, but there are some anatomical and physiological differences in men and women. The knowledge of these differences will explain why we make excellent divers on the one hand, and yet have some greater difficulties on the other.

There are many physical factors which make diving different for women than men. Let's look at some.

WOMEN HAVE LESS MUSCLE MASS PER BODY WEIGHT THAN MEN

Well, let's face it. Not only do we have a smaller muscle mass per body weight, but it is distributed differently. Unless a woman is taking male hormones or steroids, she will not develop muscles of the same size as a man. She will not develop them in the same place, either. This isn't a large problem. Diving mostly involves kicking, and we do just fine in the leg muscle area as well as in the cardiovascular area. We have the most difficulty with things requiring upper body strength and unfortunately for us, scuba is a sport involving a lot of heavy equipment.

Your full 80-cubic foot tank weighs the same 40+ pounds as does your male buddy's. You probably won't be able to lift it in the same way or with the same ease as he does, and in addition, it may not even be the appropriate size tank for you either. But if it is, there are ways to work around its weight and size. Just because your male buddy carries all his gear from the car to the beach in one trip doesn't mean you have to do the same. Don't even think about trying it, even if you are in training for the weight lifting events of the next Olympics. Arm, shoulder and back injuries from mishandling diving gear can occur and, how about saving all that energy for the dive?

The best way for women to transport heavy dive equipment is to wear it. Put that tank in the backpack, put it on your back, and wear it to the boat or the dive site. The same goes for your weight belt, and anything else heavy enough to be a problem for you to carry.

For transporting, it is easier to wear a tank than to carry it.

25

Muscle mass and fat content differ dramatically between men and women.

WOMEN HAVE A HIGHER PERCENTAGE OF BODY FAT PER BODY WEIGHT THAN DO MEN

I'm sure this extra body fat is good for something. It will help carry us through the next famine, and it certainly adds to our curvaceous figures. Since fat is less dense that muscle, it is more buoyant in the water and because of this women float better than men. But as scuba divers, who want to get BENEATH the water, it isn't all good news. It means women have to wear proportionately more weight on their belts than men. And that is literally a drag. We discuss this problem more completely in the consideration of equipment in Chapter 5.

WOMEN HAVE A GREATER SURFACE AREA TO BODY MASS RATIO

Women get colder than men, you probably already knew that. So what about all that extra body fat that is supposed to keep us warm but doesn't? Surface area to body mass ratio is a more important factor in heat retention than our slight differences in percentage of body fat.[1]

Water is a terrific heat conductor, and it conducts heat away from us whenever the water is less than 98.6° F (37° C). This means that each and every square inch of us is losing heat to the water. The smaller, thinner, or less in volume we are, the quicker we lose heat. So women tend to get cold faster.

In spite of this, one study has shown that women will endure lower body temperatures or hypothermia longer than men.[2] However being cold doesn't make for a pleasant and enjoyable dive and getting severely chilled (hypothermia) is potentially hazardous for any diver. Hypothermia causes loss of strength and dexterity. Stay warm during your dive and your buddy will not only have a fun dive, but a comfortable and safe dive.

WOMEN MAY HAVE FEWER SWEAT GLANDS PER UNIT AREA AND START SWEATING AT HIGHER TEMPERATURES THAN DO MEN

Before we all get excited about going without our antiperspirant, remember that under hot conditions you can quickly overheat. You need to plan your actions carefully in the heat. Set up your equipment *before* you put on your wetsuit. Suit up with your buddy, not in advance of your buddy. Jump into the water to cool off when you start to feel hot. If you experience a nauseous, woozy feeling while standing around in the sun with all your gear on, you may be overheated. So just cool down.

WOMEN HAVE GOOD NATURAL DEXTERITY, BALANCE, GRACE AND STAMINA

Since we are generally smaller in build with a proportionally smaller muscle mass, we may not run, swim or kick as fast. However, speed doesn't really count in diving, so this makes little difference.

Proper thermal protection is very important for women.

Women are well equipped for stamina. Women can "hit the wall" and keep on going. This is important because the distance covered or the ability to keep kicking in the face of a current is what makes a diver competent and safe. Maybe you can't swim as fast as the men with whom you dive, but if you allow yourself to 'keep on truckin' without anxiety, you'll find that you can swim just as far. Just set your own pace and don't get psyched out by the sight of your male buddy's fins disappearing ahead of you. He is being a poor buddy. Safe diving practices dictates that the faster buddy slow down and stay with his partner.

We have noticed that our female students have the grace and balance that male students lack. Women are quick to attain neutral buoyancy and keep their fins from destroying the reef. A sense of balance makes it simpler to adjust to the awkward gear worn in the water.

Smaller divers have lower air consumption rates.

WOMEN HAVE SMALLER LUNGS AND HEART, AND A HIGHER HEART RATE

Smaller lungs mean better air consumption and longer dives. The same size tank will last you a lot longer than it will an average man.

This has two major implications for you. First, analyze your diving patterns and that of your buddies'. If you return from your dives with a lot of unused air, seriously consider a smaller tank. There is no reason for dragging around a lot of air that you aren't going to use. A smaller tank is less bulky and weighs less. It is easier to carry on the beach and it is easier to kick through the water. (More on tanks in Chapter 5.) Second, many women because of their low air consumption rate can easily exceed the U.S. Navy No Decompression Table

29

limits on a single tank of air. Women therefore have to be more cautious about their bottom time because they may run out of allowable bottom time long before they run low on air, even on the first dive of the day.

WOMEN UNDER EXERTION WILL WORK CLOSER TO THEIR MAXIMUM OUTPUT

When kicking against that current, your male buddy may be working at 75% of his total capacity, while you are working at 90%. With smaller muscles, you must work harder. Under identical circumstances, a woman may be more out of breath, have a higher heart rate, become more tired, and get colder than her male partner. In other words, you may be operating closer to over-extending yourself, closer to that out-of-control feeling, closer to panic. Be conscious of the essential need to conserve strength. It's one thing to run out of steam while jogging, and quite another to run out while trying to get back to the beach through the surf zone.

Always keep something in reserve. Slow down before you get tired; you never know when the conditions may change and you must call upon your last ounce of strength.

To recap, what can you do about any physical disadvantages or difficulties we women experience in this still somewhat macho world of diving?

- Increase your knowledge of equipment and become more skilled in its selection and management (see Chapter 5).

- Increase your diving skills and know-how (see Chapters 4 and 7).

- Terminate a dive because you are COLD, no matter how upset your bigger, warmer buddy will be.

- Dress slowly, keeping cool, in warm or hot situations. Don't lug gear around after you have suited up.

- Maintain a slower pace during the dive so that you can stay well within your energy limits.

- Maintain your physical skills with regular diving; engage in aerobic conditioning and strengthening exercises year-round, so that you have a handy reserve of energy (see Chapter 4).

When Women Dive

CHAPTER FOUR

Mastering the Skills

"I only weigh 103 pounds, so I hate having to wear this 20-pound weight belt, but otherwise I just can't get down."

Petite Diver
Catalina Island, California

There are four major areas of fitness for divers: physiological, anatomical, emotional, and methodological. Let's discuss methodological. Methodological fitness means being fit in the methods of diving — in other words, our diving skills. Being skilled enhances our safety and enjoyment in the water.

There really isn't enough time available during a diving class to perfect all the skills you must learn and more advanced classes do not generally focus on basic skill development. Rather they concentrate on such subjects as deep diving, cave diving, wreck diving, night diving, search and recovery diving, underwater photography, etc.

It's up to you to continue to master the basic skills and at the same time learn new tricks of the trade. Women in particular because they have less physical strength benefit by having a higher skill level and applying the new tricks they learn.

FIN KICKS

Whether a snorkeler, skin diver and scuba diver your kick is important. A snorkeler clad only in a bathing suit may be able to get away with tiny fins and a fluttery kick, but she will be more effective and more comfortable with an improved fin kick. Any diver pushing the resistance of a wetsuit, weight belt, and a buoyancy compensator (not to mention a tank) through the water will definitely need a powerful kick.

In kicking, your power comes from the large upper thigh muscles in the front of your leg. These powerful muscles will give you the

A deep, slow kick moves you through the water with the most efficiency.

thrust you require. Too much knee action is referred to as "bicycling," and it results in the fin being moved horizontally generating little forward thrust. Concentrate on kicking from the hip rather than from the knee.

A deep, slow kick is a power kick. It will move you through the water more efficiently rate. A short, shallow kick will force you to work very, very hard to make the same headway. Make your kick as deep as you can. Concentrate on kicking your fin downward as far as you can on each stroke. If you are on the surface, visualize trying to touch the bottom as you kick. You won't actually hit the bottom, of course, unless you are in very, very shallow water. Naturally, the deeper the kick, the slower it will be. This is good; it means your fins are working at their maximum efficiency. It is counterproductive to try to move big fins quickly through the water.

In addition, concentrate on keeping fins below the surface. If your kicks coming out of the water, you are wasting energy. If you have light-weight fins, ankle weights may help (see Chapter 5). All fin kicks are more effective underwater than on the surface.

To some extent, your kick will be determined by your fin. Some of the lighter plastic fins require slightly more knee action than do the heavier rubber fins. Long flexible blades force you to make slower strokes; because of their size they simply cannot be moved rapidly.

Front Flutter Kick

The front flutter is the most common kick used both above and below the water. Done in the face-down position, it uses the large muscles on the front of your leg to provide the thrust to propel you forward. Concentrate on making each stroke count. If it takes many more than 50 kicks to cover 100 feet, your kick is not as efficient as you can make it.

Back Flutter

The back flutter kick is usually used on the surface. You lie on your back with your chin tucked in to keep water out of your snorkel. The major thrust is upward, again with the front of your leg, but you can also get power from the downstroke. This is an extremely powerful surface kick as your legs are lower in the water than in the front flutter,

Although a strong surface kick, the side flutter can be employed under water.

so you have a wider range of motion possible. It may be used as a primary surface kick or as an alternate when you are becoming tired.

Side Flutter Kick

Also primarily a surface kick, the side flutter kick is done while lying on your right side (thereby keeping your snorkel clear of the water). You must separate your fins a little so that your legs are able to travel the full range from front to back. This excellent kick allows you to see both in front of you and behind, so it is ideal for shore exits.

Frog Kick

The frog kick can be used on the surface, but its primary value is that it provides you with a means of locomotion near the bottom without stirring up sediment. From a prone position, bend your knees, separate your fins, then sweep your legs together with your fin bottoms facing each other. It sound strange, but you will find a slow frog kick to be an excellent resting kick.

Dolphin Kick

If you have not yet tried the dolphin kick, you can look forward to one of your most enjoyable underwater experiences. Both legs and feet remain together, and by undulating your body, your fins are moved jointly in a downward and upward stroke resembling the fluke motion of a dolphin or whale. Not only can this be a fast kick, but it's great fun.

Each of these fin kicks uses the muscles in your legs in different ways. Having several different kicks in your repertoire and feeling comfortable with each will provide you with alternatives when you are tired. At the first sign of leg cramps, stop, rest the muscle, massage it gently, stretch it, then change to a different kick.

What is happening to your arms during all this time? Arms are useful for many things in diving, but not for forward motion. You will tire more easily and use more air underwater if you are constantly using your arms. Avoid the habit of breast-stroking with your arms during your dive. If you have this bad habit is easy to break. Merely hold your hands clasped in front of you for a few dives and, *voila*, you will find you have ceased to swim with your arms!

Sooner or later, you will find it necessary, maybe even desirable, to kick considerable distances on the surface in order to reach your dive site or your entry/exit point. You may be faced on occasion with an unexpected current running against you, a strong wind that impedes your progress, or perhaps uncomfortably rough seas. In order to handle the distance or unanticipated events, you want to be efficient in fin kicking.

Keep your arms at your side to prevent drag and to conserve energy and air.

Surprisingly, surface swimming sometimes proves to be more difficult and more stressful than being underwater. This is one of the reasons for staying in good shape for diving. No matter what shape you are in, however, the following techniques will help.

As soon as you begin to feel taxed, slow down. Don't expect to get there as fast. You can continue to kick slowly, make headway, and conserve your strength, all at the same time. If you begin to tire, change to another type of kick. Loosen all constricting equipment or clothing, such as BC straps, wetsuit jacket and hood.

Concentrate on controlling your breathing. You must avoid becoming short of breath while in the water. You cannot let an out-of-breath situation in the water continue as long as you would during a jogging session. An out-of-breath situation can escalate quickly to a panicked response, because you experience a tightness around your chest and feelings of insufficient air. You must take positive action. Force yourself to exhale fully, inhale deeply and perform that cycle at least six times (count them). By the end of the sixth breath, you should find yourself much more comfortable and more in control. There is always an alternative to panic. Remember, controlling your breathing is one important way to control or prevent panic.

EAR CLEARING

Even though ear clearing is one of the fundamental skills which you learn in scuba training, divers often continue having trouble with this skill. There are some basic steps which may help you conquer problems with ear clearing. You need to find the technique or combination of techniques that works best for you.

There are passive methods of ear clearing, like swallowing, yawning, jaw thrust, and jaw wiggle. These methods work for many divers. If they do for you, use them by all means.

The most common active method is the Valsalva maneuver. This requires gently blowing while pinching the nose and closing the mouth. You must use caution, since it is possible to blow too hard. An excellent alternative is simply pinching the nose and swallowing.

Equalize early and often; begin at the surface and continue every few feet. If you feel pain, you've gone too deep without equalizing! Try the following steps: ascend a few feet and try again; change the position of your head — tip your head all the way back, or look up at the surface, or straight ahead, or down, then try again. If it doesn't work, don't simply blow harder. If one ear doesn't cooperate, tip your head to the side so the recalcitrant ear is uppermost.

If you have continual difficulty clearing your ears or if you have changes in hearing or feelings of fullness following a dive visit a diving physician who specializes in ear, nose and throat disorders. Be gentle with your ears; they are easy to injure. Ear injury could keep you out of the water and away from the fun of diving.

GETTING BENEATH THE SURFACE

Divers spend a lot of time on the surface, going to the dive site, coming from the dive site, waiting to go down, etc. However, underwater is where we want to be. Getting beneath the surface efficiently requires a combination of proper weighting and good physical skills.

Proper weighting means that we are neutrally buoyant at 10 feet (3 meters). Therefore, we will be slightly positively buoyant on the surface. This means we float at the surface naturally even with an empty buoyancy compensator. But it also means that we have to initiate a means to get underwater.

It is a simple matter for an overweighted diver to drop beneath the surface of the water; she simply removes the air from her buoyancy compensator and sinks. Wanting to get down quickly is a very poor reason for diving in an overweighted condition. Perfecting an efficient means of getting underwater is far better than wearing too much lead for the rest of your diving life!

We float because our bodies displace water. The more of your body that is immersed, the more water will be displaced, and the better you will float. If you lift your head out of the water it provides no displacement therefore no buoyancy and you must kick to support it.

We can use this principle to our advantage. When you take a deep breath at the surface, your chest expands, you displace more water and you float. Conversely, when you exhale, your chest contracts, you displace less water and you sink. So you can assist in your descent by exhaling. That's wonderful. But since you still have to breathe while descending, keep your lung volume relatively small with a shallow inhalation, followed by a full, slow exhalation.

A feet-first descent is especially recommended for beginning divers for several reasons: you avoid disorientation, keep better track of your buddy, and it is easier to equalize your ears in a head-up position. You begin a feet-first dive from a vertical position in the water. If you begin to sink immediately after removing the air from your BC, you may be wearing more weight than necessary. When properly

A skillful diver can descend from the surface by exhaling and keeping her body in a clean, vertical line. However, do not continue to descend if you are unable to equalize the pressure in your ears.

weighted, you can start a controlled descent by simply exhaling. Keep your legs straight and together with your fins pointing down. You can further assist the descent by pushing up against the water with your hands.

SURFACE DIVES

Let's put theory in practice. You are ready to descend. Remember to place the second stage of your regulator in your mouth, and remove all the air from your BC.

Feet-First Surface Dives

If you find you are not sinking deep enough with a simple exhalation, try the "kelp dive." This dive is used on the west coast of the U.S. where a diver often needs to sink a few feet below the surface to get underneath the kelp canopy floating on the surface. Head-first dives in kelp can entangle you or your equipment.

Feet-first 'kelp' dive.

To do a kelp dive, you start with your legs spread as far apart as you can, with one leg out in front and one leg extended back. Each arm is also extended straight out from your body at your sides, perpendicular to your torso. If you quickly snap your legs together and bring your arms down to your sides, the result will be an upward motion of your torso. The idea is to get as much of your upper body as possible out of the water. Try to get as far out of the water as your waist. As a result of this upward motion you will then be able to in turn sink several feet under the water. If you then exhale and push up with your hands against the water, you will sink even more rapidly.

Even without a proper kelp dive, you can assist your descent by first kicking upward from a vertical position in the water. This will get some of your upper body out of the water, and the downward reaction will help your descent.

Head-First Surface Dives

Although not taught by some certifying agencies, head-first surface dives are the dive of choice for skin divers, and can certainly be utilized quite successfully for scuba diving as well. In fact some divers prefer a head-first surface dive. However you must be able to equalize air spaces in a head-down and/or horizontal position. If using a head-first descent you can also stop occasionally during descent and assume a head-up position, equalize, then resume your swim down.

Pike Surface Dive

The pike dive is used by divers who are moving across the surface. You bend sharply at the waist and extend your legs straight up into the air. As soon as your legs come out of the water, you are propelled

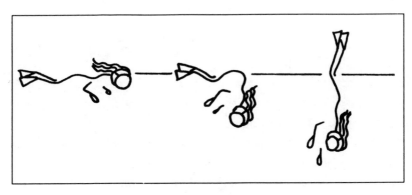

Pike surface dive.

downward head first. When your fins enter the water, start kicking down. This is a nearly effortless surface dive and can be accomplished even more easily by raising only one leg out of the water.

As soon as you turn head down, your tank may slide forward. This may be because it is improperly adjusted or the BC is too large. Both are easy problems to correct. You can also keep it from tapping the back of your head by keeping the dive gentle and smooth.

Tuck Surface Dive

The tuck dive begins from a prone position while stationary on the surface of the water. Roll forward, bringing your knees to your chest, and then extend your legs into the air. Once again, the action will sink you dramatically.

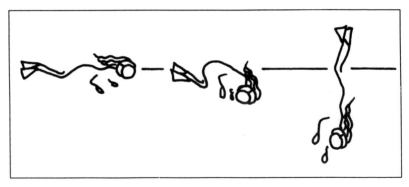

Tuck surface dive.

Whenever you are descending, feet-first or head-first, do it as quietly as possible. Of course, it feels good when you do something well, and it's nice to know you look good while doing it. More importantly, you have minimally disturbed the environment. Your surface dives should be done with as much control, grace and quiet as possible. Think of a hot knife slicing through butter. Flailing around in the water will warn the marine life for miles around that you are coming.

Buoyancy Control

The primary purpose of the buoyancy compensator (BC) is to compensate for the compression of your wetsuit at depth, thereby allowing you to maintain neutral buoyancy regardless of depth.

While many BC's are capable of enormous amounts of lift, they are not intended to support an overweighted diver, or a newly found anchor, or a chest of long lost treasure! If you are wearing a wetsuit and are overweighted at the surface, your condition will become progressively worse as you descend. Your BC may even eventually fail to give you enough lift.

BC's have made diving much simpler, but there are some specific concepts to their use. Air is lighter than water, of course, so it rises to whichever part of the BC is at the top. Please remember that the air outlet must be in the highest position in the water or you will be unable to effectively vent any air from the BC. This usually means that for most BC's you must be in an upright position, dipping your right shoulder to make your left shoulder highest, and holding the air hose high while depressing the exhaust button. Incomplete emptying when surface diving can create the frustrating and highly embarrassing situation of you frantically trying to get down, your fins whipping around like windmills in the air, and you not going anywhere! Some BC's have a release valve high on the rear of the shoulder or at the waist, thereby enabling you to vent air in a horizontal, face-down position. The ability to vent air in this position is especially convenient underwater.

During your descents, you must add air to your BC as your wetsuit compresses. A skilled diver will control buoyancy throughout the descent and *arrive* at the bottom neutrally buoyant. This is infinitely better than having an out-of-control descent which does not allow time for ear equalization, time to become acclimatized to the increasing pressure, nor time to check one's depth..

Once you arrive at the bottom, you must either add or subtract some air each time you change your depth. A skilled diver makes corrections to her BC early so that she remains neutrally buoyant at all times. You must practice this skill. Once this skill is mastered, you'll enjoy one of the greatest thrills diving has to offer; that of being neutrally buoyant and essentially free from gravity.

If the changes in depth are small, you can control your buoyancy by varying the amount of air in your lungs. You should not hold your breath, but deep, full inhalations will make you rise, and long, complete exhalations will make you sink. The use of lung volume for buoyancy control for minor changes in depth is easier than constantly changing the amount of air in the BC and is a skill worth mastering.

Each time you ascend, even a foot or two, you become buoyant as your wetsuit and the air in your BC expands in response to the reduced pressure. If you neglect to exhaust expanding air from your BC, the rapidly increasing positive buoyancy will lift you to the surface much faster than the maximum recommended ascent rate.

Your rate of ascent is of vital importance. Some research shows that we may actually be safer if we reduce ascent rates to one-half or even one-third of the U.S. Navy Dive Tables recommendation of 60 feet (18 meters) per minute. Electronic dive computers have reduced ascent rates built into their programs. We would do ourselves a great service if we take 2 or even 3 minutes to reach the surface from 60 feet. This means we must be very skilled at buoyancy control. The air must

Skillful use of the BC enables you to be weightless regardless of depth.

be vented from our BC's early and often to prevent a too-rapid ascent, and we must be able to stop in open water for three to five minutes at 10 to 15 feet (3 to 5 meters) for a safety stop.

Prior to the invention of the BC, divers got along pretty well by predetermining the depth they intended to dive and weighting themselves accordingly. They made minor adjustments in their buoyancy during the dive by changing the amount of air in their lungs. You will still see some divers choosing to dive in this manner today. It allows the divers to experience a light and "free" feeling. These divers weight themselves very lightly, and must kick down to the designated depth. If positive buoyancy is needed in an emergency, one merely drops the weight belt. This practice, however, may eliminate the ability to make a safety stop without holding on to a weighted line.

Strictly speaking, if you dive without a wetsuit, then your buoyancy should be the same at whatever depth you dive. If you are weighted properly at the surface, your buoyancy will be correct throughout the dive. You may vary it with lung volume. However, most charter boats and resorts will still require the use of a BC. They want you to have a resting station on the surface, so you will probably not be allowed in the water without a BC. All certifying agencies require you to use a BC during training regardless of whether you use a wetsuit or not.

It is still controversial in some areas as to whether you need to wear a BC with a dry suit. The anti-BC argument is that you add enough air to your dry suit to stay neutral, so a BC is redundant. The pro-BC argument maintains that the dry suit should have only enough air for comfort and not be used to provide additional buoyancy beyond equalizing squeeze unless an emergency situation arises. If a non-neoprene dry suit should fail and become filled with water, the BC could be used as a means to achieve positive buoyancy to reach the surface. Dry suits full of air also do not work well for surface swimming. When snorkeling, you will encounter less drag from a moderately filled BC than an over-inflated dry suit.

While underwater, a properly weighted, skillful diver swims in a trim, completely horizontal manner. An overly weighted diver swims at an angle to the bottom, with feet and fins quite a bit lower than head and upper body because of an overloaded weight belt and greatly inflated BC. This position creates more drag. This angle also makes it difficult to keep fins off the reef, and the diver will be inclined (no pun intended) to leave a trail of disturbed sediment behind her wherever she goes. This is both unsightly and harmful to the reef.

Although not strictly necessary when diving without a compressible wetsuit, the use of the BC is required by many dive establishments.

In summary, maintaining physical skills with regular diving, aerobic conditioning and strengthening exercises year-round will ensure a welcome reserve of "oomph" in the water. Attaining the highest skill levels possible in buoyancy control, surface dives, proper body position, entries and exits, kicks, and all the rest will add immensely to your diving confidence and pleasure.

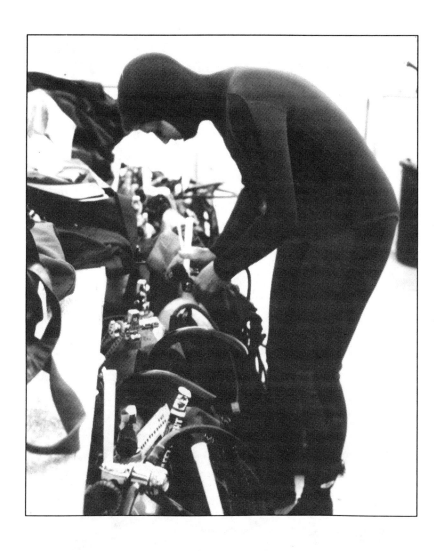

CHAPTER FIVE

You and Your Equipment

"I knew exactly what kind of fins I wanted, so I went to the dive shop to buy them. I was a complete stranger, but the owner tried to talk me out of them anyway — he said the fins would be too hard for me to kick."

Vickie Allen-Wopat
Studio City, California

The sports of skin and scuba diving are equipment intensive, each piece of diving gear with its own idiosyncrasies. There are so many things to take into consideration that it can seem overwhelming both to new and to already-certified divers. If you are new to these sports, this chapter will help. If you are already a diver, problems with your equipment may already be causing you too many hassles. Let's take a look at how you can become more comfortable and become better friends with your equipment.

In years past, one of the major problems facing women was the lack of properly sized equipment. Recently, however, diving equipment

Your mask is your window to the underwater world. It should fit properly and be comfortable.

manufacturers have been courting the attentions of their smaller and/or female customers by supplying equipment in a wide variety of sizes. A lot of attention is currently being paid to color and color coordination. Although it's great to be able to get decked out in lavender or hot pink from head to toe, don't lose sight of comfort and performance! You will still be wearing that same equipment long after the color fades (or long after you're sick of hot pink), so choose carefully. We all know our original investment in dive gear is expensive so we want to be happy with it for a long, long time. You may already own several pieces of equipment. If so, don't hesitate to critique them from the standpoint of comfort, because an additional purchase may go a long way toward improving your diving pleasure.

MASKS

Does your mask fit or leak? It is annoying to have a leaky mask, and it need not be tolerated. You can find one that fits you well. Don't get discouraged when your local dive store doesn't have what you want. There are many equipment manufacturers, and no single dive store represents them all. It is advantageous to investigate several stores for any piece of gear you need; you don't have to settle for your second choice.

Does your nose fit the nosepocket? To facilitate equalizing (see Chapter 4) a smaller nosepocket may make it easier to reach your nose with gloves on. Does your mask irritate your face or feel uncomfortable after a short time in the water? You may have a good seal, but a poorly fitting mask. Perhaps the rubber or silicone is too hard for delicate skin. Maybe you have your mask strap adjusted too tightly – many divers do. Your strap should simply hold the mask in place, not provide the water seal. Remember to re-adjust the head strap when you wear a hood.

Do you have 20/20 vision or could you use a little help? There are several companies offering pop-in correcting lenses for various styles of masks. So you are virtually assured of finding a vision correcting

*A mask fitted with prescription lenses is one option
for divers needing vision correction.*

mask which fits. However, you can also have lenses ground to your
personal prescription and bonded to the faceplate of your mask.

Many people wear contact lenses to correct vision problems. You
can dive in contacts but it is suggested that they be either soft lenses or
gas permeable hard lenses. If your correction is substantial, you will
probably find this more convenient than wearing a prescription mask
underwater and being "blind" on land until you can get to your glasses.
(You can however wear your mask on the beach or boat until your
glasses are in hand.) We dive in our soft contact lenses, and find it
preferable to diving with a prescription mask.

Many contact wearers worry about losing their contacts if their
mask floods; yet even a full flood can be managed by simply closing
your eyes. Also, soft lenses do not seem to come out in salt water if
you squint. We do not suggest going through entry-level pool training
with your contact lenses as there are many drills to be performed with-

out a mask. Your instructor can inform you when it is convenient to wear your lenses.

SNORKELS

Does your snorkel irritate your gums? A small mouth calls for a small mouthpiece on your snorkel. It's certainly uncomfortable if your mouthpiece leaks water, or if you find it difficult to clear all the water from the snorkel. The mouthpiece could cause irritation if the material is not soft enough for your mouth or if the flanges are too large. The angle of the snorkel in your mouth may also irritate. Perhaps all that is needed is a simple adjustment of the placement on your mask strap. The snorkel keeper may be too high or too low on the snorkel itself, or the keeper may be set too far along the mask strap or too close.

Your snorkel should be the right size and shape for you. The tube must be large enough in diameter for you to get enough air during exertion, but not so large that you have difficulty clearing it of water. Also, the angle of the curve should not be too sharp as this makes breathing more difficult. Don't forget that a purge valve on the snorkel makes it far easier to clear the snorkel. This can be important when you are working hard in the water. A snorkel is a relatively inexpensive piece of gear, but proper selection can make an enormous difference in your comfort and security.

FINS

All fins are not created equal. The first question to answer is whether to buy full-foot pocket fins or the adjustable heel strap type that requires the use of a bootie. Generally speaking, the larger, more powerful fins are the adjustable heel strap type. Often, the full-foot pocket fins are more generally suited to casual snorkeling. It is important to purchase fins that fit, so take along your booties when you are shopping for fins.

Next, consider the blade size and stiffness. If you purchased your fins before your first class, you probably didn't have much opportunity to try out different types of fins in the water. We discovered, while getting in condition for the physical skills required by our instructor training course, that certain fins can make a tremendous difference. Research at the State University of New York at Buffalo shows that women used less energy while kicking with a smaller, very flexible, vented fin. [3] However, research at Simon Fraser University, Canada, and more recently at UCLA, California, showed that a larger fin provides a great more thrust for less work expended than a smaller, more flexible fin.[4,5] This is important to all divers. The lower you can keep your heart rate and air consumption, the better you will feel and the more efficient you will be in the water. It's like having better gearing on your bicycle.

Your choice of fins can make an enormous difference in the power of your kick.

You want your legs to get stronger so they can take you where you want to go. Buying the softest fins you can find won't accomplish this. Some of the most colorful fins are soft and easy to kick, but do not provide much power when you need it. Following the advice of a sales person may not be in your best interest, either. They often don't seem to believe that a woman will need to do any serious kicking, or that she may want to travel efficiently through the water. Watch serious divers, instructors, or divemasters. See which fins they wear, and ask their opinion.

WETSUITS

Cooler, temperate waters have some of the most exciting diving in the world. However, women get colder than men because their smaller muscles don't generate as much heat and their smaller bodies lose heat more rapidly. The areas of greatest heat loss are our head/neck region and our torso. Wetsuits make temperate water diving more comfortable. A good wetsuit keeps you warmer in cold water than a down parka on a ski lift. So, where your wetsuit is concerned, do not compromise on fit, warmth and comfort. Your suit must fit properly and be

Wetsuits allow you to enjoy yourself in chilly waters.

of adequate thickness for the area in which you dive. Don't cheat yourself here or you'll be miserable.

A wetsuit is designed to allow a thin layer of water to become trapped between you and your suit. Your body warms this thin layer of water. The suit has to fit well. If the suit is too large, the water will slosh in and out. You will be constantly reheating cold water and will quickly become chilled.

Wetsuits are made from neoprene rubber. This rubber is filled with bubbles to achieve loft. These trapped bubbles provide the insulation. The size and content of the bubbles can determine the resilience and insulation qualities of the neoprene. Neoprene is made in varying thicknesses. In the U.S. neoprene is manufactured in fractions of an inch; other countries make neoprene in millimeters (mm). Table 5.1 will help you compare the two systems of measurement.

If the neoprene is covered only on one side with nylon or lycra, it is called "nylon 1" and the bare side is referred to as "skin." Wetsuits of this type are made "skin in" or "skin out." While "skin in" suits are warmer, they are difficult to don. You must use a powder (like baby powder or corn starch) or a detergent (like baby shampoo) to make the rubber slide across your skin.

Neoprene is most frequently covered on both sides and it is call "nylon 2". The covering may be of nylon or lycra. Lycra is shinier, available in more colors, more resistant, and more costly. Also, some manufacturers cover one side of the neoprene with a plush fabric for the inside of the suit. Plush is supposed to increase wearing comfort and help to restrict the water movement inside the suit, perhaps making the suit warmer. Today's neoprene is flexible and the covering colorful. The softest neoprene is not always the longest lasting, however, and some of the most exciting colors quickly fade. Ask about guarantees against such things as the color fading, and the covering material separating from the rubber.

Many suits are made in one piece, like a jumpsuit. Thicker suits have a jacket which is worn over separate pants. If you dive in cooler

Metric Equivalents for Inch Fractions	Table 5.1

Inches	Millimeters
1/16	1.6
1/8	3.2
3/16	4.8
1/4	6.4
5/16	8.0
3/8	9.5

waters, avoid waist-high pants, insist on farmer john pants. Farmer john's cover your upper body and shoulders and provide a double layer of protection where you need it the most.

Be certain the suit you buy is thick enough. At 60 feet (18 meters), your wetsuit will be reduced to one-half of the original thickness. If you begin the dive wearing a 1/4 inch (7 mm) suit, you will have the insulation properties of only a 1/8 inch (3 mm) suit at that depth. The type and thickness of the suit you need depends on the water temperature, of course. Table 5.2 provides you with some guidelines.

You may think you won't get chilled in tropical waters, but we have had students who have gotten quite chilled in our 90° F (32° C) swimming pool after an hour or so. Without protection, your first dive may be comfortable, but you lose heat on each dive. As the diving day wears on, and you don't fully regain your normal body temperature, you will be colder on subsequent dives.

Too many zippers will reduce the warmth of a wetsuit. Some women have trouble getting in farmer john bottoms. To facilitate easier donning of a farmer john a zipper can be added. If the suit does not come with such a zipper, have one added. The zipper can be added at the side or back of your farmer john if your jacket zipper is in the front.

As for the rest of the suit, go for warmth. Don't hesitate to have your suit modified to fit properly. If you cannot be properly fitted off the rack, spend the extra money for a custom suit, or have a stock suit modified to fit you properly. Consider extra warmth features such as attached hoods and spine pads. The attached hood in particular makes a tremendous difference in the comfort level of your dive. Another option for more thermal protection is a hooded vest.

Think FIT, WARMTH, COMFORT, and don't let anyone talk you out of it. You will regret the purchase of a "bargain" suit for the life of that suit, and for much longer than you care about the money you saved.

Exposure Suit Recommendations by Water Temperature

Table 5.2

Water Temperature	Exposure Suit
85°F (30°C) and above	Minimal insulation.
78-85°F (25-30°C)	One-piece suit of 1/8 inch (3 mm) neoprene.
70-78°F (21-25°C)	One-piece jumpsuit of 3/16 inch (5 mm) neoprene.
55-70°F (13-21°C)	Two-piece suit of 1/4 inch (7 mm) neoprene with full farmer john.
30-55°F (0-13°C)	Drysuit, with various types of underwear (dependent on temperature).

Thinner wetsuits are designed for warmer waters.

LYCRA (DIVESKINS)

A popular item in the last few years is the thin lycra suit. It was originally designed to be worn alone in warm water for protection against the "stingies," and it is most effective. Basically, a full length swimsuit, the lycra suit under a wetsuit adds a small degree of warmth. You will also appreciate the ease of dressing over a lycra suit as it provides a slick surface over which to slide your wetsuit.

Lycra suits have one drawback; the evaporation of water from a wet lycra suit can quickly chill you. So don't stand around wet. Some manufacturers have even added a barrier layer to increase thermal pro

DRY SUITS

If the water temperatures where you dive are 55° F (13° C) and below, definitely consider a dry suit. Some dry suits are made of neoprene, others of thin rubber or rubberized fabric. They all have seals to keep out the water. With fabric dry suits (shell suits) you need to wear undergarments, since the outer garment does not keep you warm. It keeps you dry. The air trapped in your undergarments provides the in-

*If you still get cold in a full, quarter-inch wetsuit,
try a drysuit.*

sulation. So the insulating properties of the undergarments you wear determines whether you will be warm or not.

As you descend, your underwear and the layer of air in the dry suit compresses, and your insulation decreases. However, unlike the wetsuit, you can add more air at depth to your dry suit and therefore restore the insulation! Generally dry suits require that you carry more weight, especially if you have thick undergarments. The extra weight is needed to counteract the positive buoyancy of the additional trapped air.

It seems to us that dry suits are still designed and cut for the male physique, but fitting may be easier because the suit doesn't have to conform to your figure as strictly as a wetsuit. Make certain it fits around the hips and that the legs are long enough. Inadequate material in the leg and crotch area will restrict your swimming ability and make it almost impossible to kneel or get up from a kneeling position. Try kneeling, crouching and touching your toes in the suit during the fitting process.

There are several kinds of dry suits and insulation available. Your choice will be made based on a series of factors, such as, prevailing water temperature, number of dives per year, type of diving, ease of repair, and maintenance requirements. You may also be strongly motivated by the cost.

Purchase a dry suit only from a establishment which provides training in its use, as dry suits require very different handling and diving techniques from wetsuits. If you live in an area with cold water, or are just tired of diving cold, consider a dry suit.

You will be a great deal warmer in a hood, gloves and booties.

BOOTS (BOOTIES)

Booties serve two purposes: as thermal protection in colder water, and as foot protection from both the environment and your fins. Booties designed for boat diving have softer soles than do those designed for divers who scramble over rocks or coral rubble. A well soled bootie adds a whole lot of comfort to your rocky beach days!

Do you have a highly arched foot? A high arch can make getting into your booties so frustrating. Shop around. Every manufacturer makes boots with a different cut, and you will find some easier to put on than others. There are also boots with zippers or with wrap-around closures. However, if you dive in cold water, remember that any opening, including zippers, means a place for warm water to leave and cold water to come in. Also, zippers may get clogged with sand when you beach dive.

GLOVES

Gloves are also designed to offer both thermal and environmental protection. When diving in warm water, consider going gloveless. Divers may actually cause reef creatures harm when we carelessly place our hands in inappropriate places. We are much more careful when diving without gloves. However if you will be making a rocky entry and need to be to grab onto the rocks without getting cut, please remember to wear your gloves even in warm waters. In moderate waters, 1/8 or 3/16 inch (3 or 5 mm) neoprene is the appropriate choice in material. Colder waters demand more thermal protection. You will need 1/4 inch (7 mm) gloves or mittens, which keep your hands warmer.

Women in general will encounter problems in finding neoprene gloves that fit. Most gloves are cut to fit men and a man's size Small just isn't right; the fingers are too short and the palms are too wide. Some brands are better for women than others. Take the time to shop.

WEIGHTS AND BELTS

The ideal amount of weight to wear is that which allows for neutral buoyancy at 10 to 15 feet (3 to 4.5 meters) of depth with a nearly empty tank. You must be able to do a safety stop at 10 to 15 feet at the end of your dive. Because they are usually more naturally buoyant, women must wear proportionally more weight than men. Sad but true, you must expend the energy required to move this weight around, whether above or under water.

Compare these two neutrally-buoyant divers at 30 feet of depth. The one on the left has so much air in her BC that it is obvious that she is extremely overweighted.

Some divers overweight themselves and justify it by stating that they just cannot get underwater otherwise, and that it doesn't really matter since one can just add air to the buoyancy compensator (BC) to achieve neutral buoyancy. Diving overweighted adds physical stress and awkwardness to your diving. Not only do you have to endure kicking that extra weight around, but you must move that overly inflated BC through the water. The increased resistance means that you will be working much harder and your air consumption will reflect that energy output. A grossly inflated BC also makes you awkward and unstable. Finally, an overweighted diver usually travels through the water at an angle rather than completely horizontal. This also causes drag and requires an increased workload..

Getting beneath the surface without being overweighted requires skills which are easy to learn. Don't be content with being overweighted simply to be pulled down from the surface by the extra weight. See Chapter 6 for the techniques you need.

Be determined to reduce the amount of weight you carry to the minimum. When we dive in a 1/4 inch (7 mm) wetsuit with a standard 71.2 cubic foot steel tank, we wear 10% of our body weight. When we dive in a 1/8 inch (3 mm) wetsuit with the same tank, we wear only 3-pound ankle weights. That feels wonderful. Even if you are not particularly lean you should also start at 10% of your weight and be miserly about adding each and every pound to your belt. You will enjoy your dives more, and finish your diving days with more energy. Remember though that different equipment will affect your buoyancy. Generally you must wear additional weight if using a standard aluminum 80 tank because they are positively buoyant at the end of the dive while a steel 63 will be negative throughout the dive.

The weights on your belt should be evenly divided and positioned just in front of your hips, or right above your hip bones. Because of the curve of your hips, it is impossible to wear your weight belt below your hip bones. You can push your belt down there, but it rarely stays put; it slides back up to your waist. Only men get away with that. Wearing two large hip weights, for example two 9-pound (4-kg) weights, means that you have 9 pounds (4 kg) pressing on each of your hip bones all day. That means sore hips tomorrow! A better solution is several smaller weights. They are comfortable, much kinder to your hips, and allow easy adjustments.

Other solutions are neoprene belts or shot-filled belts. These belts are kind to the bare hips of a diver in a swimsuit or a lycra suit. Belts constructed from neoprene usually have pockets sewn in so you can drop in weights of various sizes. However, a wetsuit wearer has ample protection, and she will have to put a little more lead onto the belt to compensate for the neoprene rubber from which the belt is constructed.

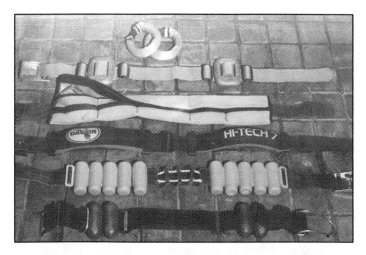

There are many choices in weight belts. Some are much more comfortable for women. From top to bottom: ankle weights; standard belt with expanding buckle; neoprene belt with pockets; adjusting belt with pre-set shot pouches; belt with expansion feature at back; rubber belt with wire buckle.

Shot-filled belts are soft and flexible, but you could have some problems. Some of these belts are too wide for a woman. There just isn't enough vertical space at your waist for the belt. Others are too long for the female waist. Often when you alter the waist length, the weight ends up too far behind you. A newer belt, Watermark's Seasoft and Dacor's Hi-Tech (made by Watermark), consists of two shot-filled tubes connected at the rear by an adjusting buckle, a definite improvement. The belt comes in pre-set weights, and intermediate weighting is provided by smaller tubes that may be added to the belt or used as ankle weights.

When wetsuits are worn, your belt should have some method of compensating for compression of your suit: rubber inserts, a rubber belt, or A compensating buckle. If the belt or buckle doesn't compensate for suit compression at depth, you will have to tighten it when you descend. If you don't, it will probably rotate, and in an emergency you may not be able to locate the quick release buckle. Remember to adjust your belt upon ascent.

Our belt of choice is a rubber belt, wire buckle, and "bullet" weights of 1 to 2 pounds (.5 to 1kg) each. This arrangement has been the most comfortable for us. Don't lose sight of your comfort and safety by skimping on your weighting system.

Another very comfortable option is to go without a weight belt and use an integrated system that contains BC, backpack, and weights in one unit. Keep in mind that with a full tank, the whole thing can weigh 60 pounds (27 kg) plus, depending on how much lead you require. Be aware that some of these systems put all the weight at your back. This tends to pull you backward in the water. One innovative system has pouches toward the front of the BC for lead shot bags. This system works well because the lead may be easily removed when moving your gear, and it is quite comfortable in the water.

ANKLE WEIGHTS

Have you noticed a nagging backache at the end of your diving day? Your back may be complaining, because when you are swimming in a horizontal position with 20 pounds around your waist, your back knows it. Do you wear fins with plastic blades? This may make it even worse. Plastic blades are lighter than black rubber and your feet tend to float up behind you, thereby putting an arch in your back. Solution? Subtract 2 or 3 pounds from your waist and transfer it to your ankles in the form of ankle weights. They feel strange at first, but your leg muscles quickly adjust, and your back will love it. Ankle weights also make it easier to kick in light plastic fins while on the surface. You could also wear heavier rubber fins.

BUOYANCY COMPENSATORS

Kudos to the manufacturers who make BC's in Extra Small and even Extra Extra Small. Finally, smaller divers can get a proper fit. However, note the length of the jacket. Does the waist band cover your weight belt? Clearly you can't have that. Does it have a cummerbund? Cummerbunds are a neat idea with a tuxedo, but when they cover your weight belt, you could have a life threatening problem.

Be choosy in your selection of a buoyancy compensator.
It is an important part of your gear.

Recently, BC manufacturers have been adding features designed to make the units more comfortable when worn with a swimsuit only. Do we hear cheers from the Florida Keys? However, wetsuit/dry suit ladies, consider carefully. All that upholstering with foam in the back, shoulders and cummerbund feels wonderful on bare skin, but you may actually have to add weight to your belt to sink your buoyancy compensator! Forget it! Some women may be already wearing close to 18% of their body weight in lead. Stick with a bladderless, unpadded

BC , or one with neutral density foam, so you can get away with the least amount of weight possible.

See the section on Weights and Belts for information on systems which combine the buoyancy compensator with your weights.

Are you beginning to get the feeling that it is beneficial to be knowledgeable with regard to dive gear? You're right! And there's more.

TANKS

There is a lot more to tanks than you might have discerned from your scuba class. You learned that there are basically two kinds of tanks: aluminum and steel. One rusts, one doesn't, one's cheaper, etc. Well, there are other aspects which are very important to you. Five of these are size, weight, capacity, working pressure, and buoyancy.

Tank Size

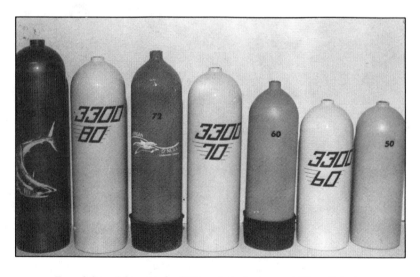

*From left to right: standard 80 cu. ft. tank; compact 80 cu. ft. tank;
standard 72 cu. ft. tank; high pressure 70 cu. ft. tank;
low pressure 60 cu. ft. tank; high pressure 60 cu. ft. tank;
standard 50 cu. ft. tank.*

Scuba Tank Capacities versus Working Pressures	Table 5.3

Tank Capacity	Working Pressure
Low Capacity 50 cu. ft. Aluminum	High Working Pressure 3000 psi
High Capacity 104 cu. ft. Steel	Low Working Pressure 2640 psi

Tanks range in length from about 20 to 30 inches (50 to 75 cm), and in diameter from 6 to 8 inches (15 to 20 cm). If you are a small diver, a large tank will bang you in the back of the head and get in the way of your legs. Also, remember your physics. The bigger the diameter of the tank, the more energy is required to move it through the water. The difference can be dramatic!

Tank Weight

Tanks vary in weight (empty, without valves) from about 23 to 40 pounds (10 to 18 kg). When full, add from 4 to 7.6 pounds (1.8 to 3.5 kg) for the air inside. Forty-seven and a half pounds (21.6 kg) is heavy. Divers often assume that aluminum tanks are lighter. Not always true. Many steel tanks are lighter than an 80 cubic foot aluminum tank. Shop with the final weight of the tank in mind.

Tank Capacity

The capacity of a U.S. tank (how much air it holds) is expressed in cubic feet (cu. ft.). Tanks on the market today range from about 15 cu. ft. to about 105 cu. ft.. The ones in most common use are 50's, 71.2's, and 80's. However, there are other sizes. Which you choose depends on your air consumption. While it is nice to have extra air, it costs energy to drag around a bigger tank than you need.

Tank Working Pressure

The working pressure is the pressure in pounds per square inch (psi) to which your tank is filled. Some tanks are high pressure tanks (3000 psi and above); others are low pressure tanks (1800 psi to about 2500 psi). A few tanks fall in the middle of the range.

A high working pressure does not mean a large capacity. Many low capacity tanks have high working pressures, and vice versa (see Table 5.3). Select a high pressure tank based on how easy it is to obtain the appropriate air fills. A tank with a working pressure of 3000 psi is full only at that pressure.

Let's say you dive with a high pressure 50 cu. ft. tank because it is short and it seemed to be the right amount of air when you dived in Cozumel. Then you board a California dive boat and your tank is filled to only 2250 psi. You now have only about 37 cu. ft. Is that enough? It could mean very short dives. However, a standard low pressure 71.2 cu. ft. steel tank at the same pressure (though 6 inches longer) would have about 65 cu. ft. of air. Quite a difference!

Sample Scuba Tank Buoyancies		Table 5.4
Tank	**Buoyancy Full**	**Buoyancy Empty**
Standard Aluminum 80	-1.0 lbs	+4.1 lbs
Slim Steel 71.4	-7.6 lbs	-2.3 lbs

Table 5.5

Scuba Tank Specifications

Information Taken from Published Manufacturers Data†						
Type	Capacity (Cu. Ft.)	Top Working Pressure (PSI)	Length (In.)	Diameter (In.)	Weight (Lbs.)	Buoyancy Empty Seawater (Lbs.)
Alum.	50	3000	18.7	7.3	25.1	+0.3
Alum.	53	3000	19.1	7.3	28.3	-1.6
Steel	60.6	3300	22.0	6.0	22.7	-2.5
Alum.	67	3000	23.0	7.3	32.8	-0.3
Steel††	71.2	2475	25.0	6.8	29.5	+1.8
Steel	71.4	3300	20.5	6.8	29.4	-5.7
Steel	71.4	3300	25.4	6.0	26.0	-2.3
Steel	75.8	2640	26.2	6.8	31.0	-0.1
Alum.†††	80	3000	27.0	7.3	34.5	+4.1
Alum.	80	3000	26.1	7.3	36.0	+0.9
Steel	80.6	3500	19.7	7.3	27	-1.0
Steel	95.1	2640	23.8	8.0	38.2	+0.6
Alum.	100	3000	26.1	8.0	44.0	+2.0
Steel	100	3500	23.9	7.25	33.0	0.0

† Figures rounded to one decimal place
†† Standard 71.2 cu. ft. steel tank.
††† Standard 80 cu. ft. aluminum tank.

Even the smaller 60 cu. ft. tank looks large on this average-sized female diver.

Tank Buoyancy

The buoyancy of your tank is one of the most important factors to you. Do not let the sales person off the hook; do not sign any sales slip until you see the figures for the buoyancy of the tank. The negative values in Table 5.4 mean that the tank is negatively buoyant and will sink. Positive values mean that the tank is positively buoyant and will float. The standard aluminum tank sinks when full but floats when empty or near empty. When you use a positively buoyant tank, you must add weight to your belt to compensate for it. Otherwise, you will not be able to do a safety stop at 10 feet (3 meters) with your tank at 600 psi. However, with a negatively buoyant tank, you actually get to remove a few pounds from your belt. Yeah! Remember that a negatively buoyant tank is not necessarily heavier above water; in some cases they are actually lighter than buoyant tanks.

Manufacturers have been aware of the difficulties imposed by positively buoyant tanks. The newest aluminum tanks on the market are designed to be negatively buoyant when full and near neutral when empty, eliminating the need to add the extra weight.

Do not attempt to carry a tank by the valve for any distance.

What's the bottom line? Let's say you are 5'1", weigh 104 pounds and dive mostly in southern California. A good choice could be a negatively buoyant, 60 cu. ft. pressure steel tank, or you may want to look at the newer, smaller doubles. Table 5.5 provides manufacturers data on some common tanks to help you choose wisely.

REGULATOR

The United States Navy had done comparative studies of various regulators. Ask to see the Navy ratings if available on the model of regulator you select. Purchase the highest rated regulator you can af-

A cart makes gear hauling a manageable task.

ford. The models in the top of the line from each manufacturer should give you dependability, breathing ease and reasonable maintenance.

Remember those sore gums from a poorly fitted snorkel? The same can happen with a poorly fitted second stage mouthpiece (The first stage is the part that fits on the tank, the second stage is the part from which you breathe). Have your dive shop get you a mouthpiece that fits. There are new mouthpiece designs that eliminate gum and jaw discomfort. If you have a small mouth, you may even find one of the new lighter second stages more comfortable.

GEAR BAG

Be realistic about the size of your gear bag. Get one no longer than is necessary to hold your gear. A large bag spreads the weight over a large area and is hard to carry, especially when full. The closer you can get the weight of the bag to your center of gravity, the easier to carry, so insist on a shoulder strap. Also, consider a model you can wear like a backpack, or one that has built-in wheels.

GEAR MANAGEMENT

Resist any impulse to muscle your gear around. In lifting, use your legs, not your back. A single injury can spoil the appeal of diving for you. Stress-free loading/unloading is possible if you wear your tank/BC and weight belt for one trip and your gear bag (especially when wet) on another.

No need to get jealous when you see divers wheeling their gear around in a nifty cart. There are several innovative ones on the market, so why not join them? It will definitely improve your outlook when it comes to transporting your gear. Everyone will admire your intelligence when you move your gear with such ease.

In summary, your diving experience can be greatly enhanced by critically examining your dive gear to be sure everything possible is done to ensure fit and comfort. Your smaller muscles not only do not generate much heat, but they make it difficult to handle heavy gear. You are special, and you have special requirements. Treat yourself to carefully selected and modified dive gear. Your enjoyment will increase and you'll have more energy. After all, you're worth it.

When Women Dive

CHAPTER SIX

Staying Healthy

"Based on current statistics, it is accurate to state that recreational diving is a safe sport today."

Susan Innes
Instructor, Attorney

It seems hard to believe, but even today, at the end of the 20th century, in this age of feminine pilots, astronauts, commercial divers, dual-income households, and female family heads, most physiological questions about the effects of diving on females remain unanswered. Researchers have gathered much information (there are many theories, some studies, and a few surveys from actual female divers) but the quest goes on for definitive answers to almost all queries.

In 1986, the Undersea and Hyperbaric Medical Society (UHMS) held its 35th Workshop. It was devoted to "Women in Diving"[6]. The proceedings were published and much of what follows is information shared by the participating authorities, and reflects the authorities thinking on this subject so dear to all women who dive.

Let's consider some questions frequently asked by female divers.

Women have special physiological concerns while diving.

AM I MORE LIKELY TO GET DECOMPRESSION SICKNESS (DCS)?

We've come almost full circle on this one. In the beginning, the U.S. Navy Decompression dive tables were developed using men as models, and most military men are young and fit. Women began counting themselves in as pilots, divers, and other professionals subject to pressure changes. They began to go where the men went, as doctors, nurses, attendants, technicians, etc. So the question arose: since males and females are quite different, might it be that we would respond to pressure changes differently?

Dr. Bruce Bassett originally examined the U.S. Air Force School of Aerospace Medicine altitude training records in 1973.[7] He had reason to re-examine these records recently, and continued to find a greater incidence of decompression sickness in women than in men.[8] However, the backgrounds of the people varied. The males in the study were flight personnel who would be expected to have undergone many high altitude training flights. The females were nurses in flight training. When a group of male Air Force Academy cadets underwent the same kind of training, they showed similar frequency of decompression sickness cases as the women.

Dr. Susan Bangasser's Medical Aspects of the Woman Diver Survey asked respondents to answer inquiries on their personal experience with DCS.[9] She utilized the returned surveys from 649 women sport divers in the U.S., Caribbean, and a few other countries. She uncovered 29 cases of DCS occurring out of 88,000 dives. In order to evaluate this material further, Dr. Bangasser attempted to set up a control group. Her female respondents in the Instructor category (divemasters, assistant instructors and instructors) were responsible for half of these dives, or approximately 44,000. She conducted a survey of male instructors (similar group) and had respondents with a total of 43,000 dives. This male group had a much lower reported incidence of DCS than did the females. The female instructors showed a .023% incidence of DCS, while their male counterparts suffered only a .007%. It must be pre-

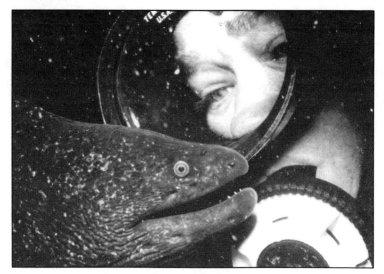

*The number of women in the diving profession
has risen dramatically in the last decade.*

sumed that all replying persons were honest when filling out the questionnaires.

The Bangasser and Air Force studies indicated that women were more susceptible to DCS than men. Researchers found a few reasons to question these studies, but dive instructors heeded their findings and have been cautioning their female divers to be more conservative. (Indeed, we all need to be cautious when using the U.S. Navy Decompression and No Decompression Tables for few of us fit the profile of the masculine, strong, young and fit Navy diver.)

A recent paper entitled "Decompression Sickness in Women Divers" contains information taken from diving log data at the Naval Diving and Salvage Training Center (NDSTC) in Florida.[10] Twenty-eight female students were compared to 487 male classmates on 878 air and mixed-gas dives between 120 and 300 feet (36.5 and 91 meters) of sea water. All bottom times were less than 20 minutes (remember, decompression stops are not considered bottom time, but part of ascent time). *"None of the women experienced DCS while eight men devel-*

oped DCS symptoms." This kind of information is certainly worthy of further study.

The data from the Navy Training Center suggests that female divers are at no greater risk from DCS than their male buddies under similar dive profiles. However, it must be kept in mind that these dives were all deep dives of relatively short duration.

Women average 10-25% body fat content, noticeably higher than men's.[11] Fat differs from other tissues where nitrogen is concerned. Fat absorbs nitrogen more slowly, holds up to 5 times more, and releases it more slowly. These fatty tissues are not as effected by short, deep dives as they are by dives of longer duration. It appears that women making the same short, deep dives as men will have comparable opportunities of contracting the dreaded "bends" – not more. This is certainly good news!

A word of caution, however. The Bassett and Bangasser studies both showed women with a better chance of getting "bent." A possible explanation for this discrepancy relates to longer dives and repetitive dives. The Zwingelberg report states "The physiologic difference between short and long-duration dives may very well explain why women at NDSTC are not at a greater risk of sustaining diving-related DCS than men." But the report goes on to say "Saturation, experimental and multiple repetitive dives may prove to be different situations . . . a greater percentage of body fat correlates positively with a higher susceptibility to DCS." Since women ordinarily are capable of longer bottom times because of their anatomy and physiology, it seems reasonable to suggest that this is why Dr. Bangasser found a higher rate of DCS in women than in men. As the Zwingelberg report says, "This question is not likely to be settled until more women have completed enough long-duration . . . dives to permit analysis."[10]

The U.S. Navy Dive Tables are based on six theoretical tissue compartments, ranging from fast to slow compartments. Hypothetically, there are an infinite number of tissue types in each of us. The central nervous system and the muscles are often referred to as possible examples of fast tissues that take up and release nitrogen quickly. Fatty tissue, bone marrow, and joints are often referred to as possible examples of slow tissues that take up and release nitrogen. In actuality no particular tissue in the body correlates with any compartment used in the model.

One new set of tables has eliminated some of the slower compartment in the calculations for repetitive dives, while some of the dive computers have doubled the number of compartments taken into consideration. We, the authors, feel safer when more compartments are involved in designing tables and/or dive computers. It is important to ask about the number of compartments used in the respective model used when selecting tables and dive computers. One clue is the amount of time it takes to "go off" the tables. Most computers require 24 to 48 hours before you are considered returned to your pre-dive condition, while one set of tables requires only six. This is an enormous difference.

Until the Bangasser survey, there was nothing to tell us if women were getting "bent" at a particular time, for example, during their periods or while using birth control pills. It has been suggested that since birth control pills are associated with circulation problems, there might be an increased risk while using this medication. During a woman's menstrual cycle there is increased fluid retention and, again, this may influence circulation. Reduced circulation has been associated with a greater risk of DCS. However, Dr. Susan Bangasser reports, "It appears that the percentage of women who have had decompression sickness on a decompression dive under the studied conditions (during menstrual period and on birth control pills) does not differ from the percentage achieved by women not on the pill". Also, the percentage of women "bent" during no-decompression dives while on the pill or during their period was not significantly different from the percentage "bent" during decompression dives.

Today, by using a Doppler machine it is possible to detect bubbles in a diver's bloodstream after a dive. We would expect bubbles to be found in divers needing decompression. However, Karl Huggins of the University of Michigan conducted a study and reported that bubbles were present in all cases of divers making dives to the no-decompression limits of the U.S. Navy dive tables (even though they did not exceed the limit!)[12] This study points out the necessity of using the tables conservatively and avoiding dives to the no-decompression limits. Special tables have been developed using new conservative limits and have formed the basis for the development of the first commercially successful dive computer.

The latest research indicates that your rate of ascent is of critical consequence. A rapid ascent may cause DCS even if the length and depth of the dive are properly conservative. Slow your ascent rate to 40 or even 20 feet per minute (12 to 6 meters per minute) especially in shallow water and you will be far safer. The Undersea and Hyperbaric Medical Society recommends stopping your ascent at 10 to 15 feet (3 to 4.5 meters) for 3 to 5 minutes. This will still further lessen the chances of decompression sickness. These safety stops have been shown to make an enormous difference.

CAUTION: The U.S. Navy Tables were not designed for dives which are cold or strenuous. We breathe in more air, therefore more nitrogen, when we are cold and when we are working hard. The Navy recommends that we use the next greater time scheduled (move up one letter group) following a dive that is cold or one that is strenuous.[13] If it is both cold and strenuous, it makes sense to go up two letter groups.

WHAT IF I GET PREGNANT?

The question of whether to dive while pregnant is of considerable concern to many female divers. However else it affects your lifestyle, the definitive word is: DON'T. Don't dive while you are pregnant. To be honest, we feel this advice is often given as a 'safe' solution to a currently unanswered question. The question: Will I, and my baby, be safe while diving with he/she still in my womb? The answer: Nobody really knows. In the liability-conscious U.S., the answer must be "no" until we all know more.

What about possible birth defects? While there are many women who have dived safely while pregnant, certain studies indicate that there could be a problem — if not with the mother, then with the baby. Dr. Susan Bangasser, co-author of the 1979 book, "Women Underwater," dived safely while pregnant with both her children.[14] Dr. Eugenie Clark, world famous marine biologist, also reported diving safely during her pregnancies.[15] However, Dr. Bangasser cautions that she limited her diving to shallower than 30 feet (9 meters) and recommends that this is certainly not the time to learn diving.

Divers do well to utilize all the recommended safety measures.

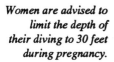

Women are advised to limit the depth of their diving to 30 feet during pregnancy.

In Dr. Bangasser's 1978 survey of 72 pregnant women, all of whom dived during pregnancy, revealed no associated birth defects.[9] Another survey, by Margie Bolton in 1980, seemed to indicate that diving could be blamed for some incidence of birth defects. Of 136 women who reported diving while pregnant, six children were born with birth defects; two of these women reported dives to depths in excess of 100 feet (30 meters).[16] This degree of incidence may not be greater than the incidence in the general population, however this survey also showed a larger proportion of complications.

Additional studies using animals as test subjects have been conducted. The Gilman study in 1982 using hamsters provided evidence that diving does cause birth defects,[17] while the Bolton & Alamo (1981) experiment with rats showed none.[18] This was also the conclusion of the Bolton-Klug study in 1983 using sheep.[19]

Dr. Edward Lanphier, University of Wisconsin, presented a "Pregnancy and Diving" paper at the UHMS Workshop. He concluded, "For the present, we must assume that diving can increase the incidence of birth defects".[20]

In addition to the possibility of birth defects, there exist other potential dangers. Does my unborn baby run a greater risk of decompression sickness (DCS) than I do? Again, no one knows for sure, but at least one study has indicated that the unborn child may be less susceptible to decompression sickness than the mother. However, this information does not tell us that a dive free from DCS for the mother will be safe for the baby. There is more than one reason to suspect that ANY bubbles forming for ANY reason in a fetus may result in a life-endangering situation. Any pregnant woman contracting decompression sickness late in her term runs an increased risk of giving birth to a stillborn child.[20]

Obviously every diver, pregnant or not, will attempt to avoid DCS. The problem facing a pregnant woman with DCS symptoms is that the fetus may very well be in additional danger from the cure. Oxygen therapy is part of the treatment given in the recompression chamber, and certainly increased oxygen pressure results in added dangers for an unborn child. This provides further argument for limiting any dives to a depth shallower than 30 feet (9 meters), if one chooses to dive at all.

Dr. Lanphier says, "It is the individual woman's responsibility to decide whether to dive during pregnancy or not, and she deserves to have 'the facts,' such as they are. At the same time, it seems incumbent upon professional people to have a considered opinion and to express it." [20]

On the other hand, the Undersea and Hyperbaric Medical Society has recommended "No scuba diving deeper than 30 feet, and avoidance of decompression diving." [5]

Women make excellent divers. Natural grace, dexterity and balance go a long way underwater. With the ranks of sport and professional female divers rapidly increasing, it is necessary to more accurately gauge any dangers associated with being a female diver and to establish more guidelines. It is an easy thing to say — don't dive for the nine months of your pregnancy. However, we are cautioned about our diving while we are attempting to get pregnant, and advised not to dive for a couple of months after giving birth. This amounts to a full year out of the water for each and every child a woman bears. That's a lot of time for our marine biologists, instructors, photographers, divemasters, military personnel, travel specialists, film industry persons, hyperbaric medical personnel, commercial divers and all the other women making a living in dive-related activities, not to mention all the hundreds of thousands of women all over the world who dive for the sheer love of it. We all need more concrete information on which to base our decisions.

The choice is yours. Additional things to take into consideration if you dive while you are pregnant are:

1. Certainly morning sickness would contribute to any tendency toward motion sickness and it is advised to not use seasickness medication while pregnant.

2. Sinus drugs may not be safe to take while pregnant.

3. Never dive if you are ill. Check with your physician.

4. You are less fit and tire more easily. So avoid heavy surf, currents and strenuous dives.

5. Avoid risk of hypothermia and chilling.

6. Limit the depth and duration of your dives.

7. Consider limiting the depth of your dives while you are attempting to become pregnant. It usually takes some weeks to discover whether you are actually pregnant, and it would be worrisome to discover you are pregnant AFTER you had made a deep dive.

8. You may have reduced breathing function; make sure you don't get into an out-of-breath situation.

9. Be careful how and what you lift.

10. There may be an increased risk of decompression sickness for the mother due to fluid retention. (One set of guidelines indicates reducing the U.S. Navy No-Decompression limits by one-half.)

11. There will be quite a few physical problems encountered: wetsuits won't fit; weight belts are difficult to wear (if at all); people will look at you funny (again!); where does the waist strap go?

12. Always consult a physician familiar with diving for advice, guidelines and current information.

IS IT OKAY TO DIVE DURING MY PERIOD? WHAT ABOUT SHARKS?

Most women do not interrupt their ordinary activities during their menstrual period. There is no reason to curtail your diving activity if you feel well. Some women have noticed that menstrual cramps appear to subside during and following a dive. Other female divers have reported feeling colder, and it is common to generally feel less energetic during this time. It is certainly much more comfortable to wear internal protection (tampons) than external (napkins).

There is absolutely no evidence whatsoever to lead one to believe that menstrual blood attracts sharks. Menstrual flow is made up of water, mucus and hemolyzed (old) blood. Sharks may be attracted to fresh blood, but not to menstrual blood.[14] Also, the total amount of blood is small and the amount of leakage during a dive while wearing a tampon would be very small. It takes a lot more chumming to bring sharks in. Sharks appear to be attracted to movement of a certain type, most likely the type of movement mimicking that of a sick or injured prey.

It is more common to see divers chasing sharks around than vice-versa.

Statistically, shark attacks are extremely rare. It is more appropriate to be concerned about buckling your seat belt while driving to your dive site than to worry about sharks (in the water).

WILL MY METHOD OF BIRTH CONTROL AFFECT MY DIVING?

There has been speculation that birth control pills increase your risk of decompression sickness because they affect blood circulation. There is no evidence to support this theory, but it pays to be on the safe side. Discuss the selection and side effects of your birth control pills with your physician, and be, as always, conservative in your dive profile.

There have been no reported difficulties with I.U.D.'s, diaphragms, and foams. Avoid diving with anything that would create an artificial air space that could not be equalized. A cervical cap is such a device. Who knows what type of squeeze could develop!

It is essential for all divers to carefully monitor the depth and duration of each dive.

I INTEND TO DIVE THE REST OF MY LIFE. WILL I HAVE ANY PROBLEMS AFTER MIDDLE AGE?

Dr. Eugenie Clark expressed some concern with this question during the 1986 UHMS Workshop.[6] During a discussion following the conference she asked if there were any guidelines on diving with osteoporosis. This condition affects some people (especially women) more than others and is caused by age-related loss of calcium from the bones, resulting in decreased bone density. No one participating in this discussion indicated having any information on the effects of diving on bone density. However, since it has long been shown that some commercial divers display a porosity of the bone called dysbaric osteonecrosis, it is a real concern to women who may also have osteoporosis.

Research has shown that a slow ascent rate and safety stops are extremely beneficial in preventing decompression sickness.

As far as we know, dysbaric osteonecrosis is rare in sport divers who dive conservatively, but divers are concerned about the effect of years of diving on their bodies. Dysbaric osteonecrosis is associated with years of decompression diving. As we mentioned earlier, even being close to the no-decompression limits may result in some bubble formation, and bubble formation within bone tissue is certainly to be avoided.

Aside from bone loss, there is the suspicion that middle-aged and older divers are more susceptible to decompression sickness than are younger divers. Recent DAN Doppler studies revealed that women 40 or over were more likely to have detectable bubbles on dives 80 feet or greater.[21] This is one more reason to exercise constraint by staying well within the limits and making safety stops on all dives.

Diving keeps women of all ages active and involved.

Diving is one of those sports that can be enjoyed well into our older years. It certainly helps to stay physically fit and to have a physical every year. Most of us have no intention of ever giving up diving! This means we have to stay safe and in condition, but we would want to do that anyway, right?

WHAT IS THE PROPER NUTRITION FOR A DIVER?

Any working body needs to be regularly fueled. Since diving tends to be an early morning activity, the meal you have the night before is important. It should be a well-balanced meal containing protein and carbohydrates. As the diving day continues, your depleted energy needs to be renewed by food. Just as a backpacker needs regular sustenance, so does a diver.

Although our sport seems effortless at times, we are indeed requiring a great deal from our muscles and tissues. Stay away from junk food and empty calories. The short-term boost in energy is not worth what they do to your figure. Besides, divers benefit more from the long-term energy supply offered by nutritious foods. Avoid gassy and greasy foods, as well as carbonated drinks. Changes in pressure while underwater could cause discomfort in your stomach and intestines if you have a lot of gas.

Every exhalation while breathing on scuba represents loss of fluids from your body. Unless you make a concerted effort to replace this lost fluid during your diving day, you may end up dehydrated. Being dehydrated could make you more susceptible to decompression sickness. Keep yourself hydrated by drinking lots of water and non-caffeinated beverages before and between dives.

CAN I SAFELY DIVE WHILE ON MEDICATION?

In many instances the answer is NO! It is not safe to dive on some medications. Many prescription drugs have side effects that are greatly exaggerated under pressure, and many drugs have properties that alter the way in which you perceive reality: they may cause drowsiness, vertigo, dizziness, etc. It is generally recommended not to dive while using sedatives, tranquilizers, antidepressants, antihistamines, hypoglycemic medicines, any heart medication, asthma or bronchitis medicines and anticonvulsants. Exercise caution in using some anti-inflammatory or anti-hypertensive medications. You must check with your physician before diving on any drug. If he or she is unfamiliar with what pressure changes may do to you, continue to seek information from those more knowledgeable, perhaps a physician with dive medicine experience.

Don't blithely go diving under the influence of any drug without having full knowledge of possible side effects. Even over-the-counter remedies may have undesirable side effects. For instance, antihistamines are known to cause drowsiness. Usually considered safe is the sustained action form of Sudafed® and nasal sprays, most antibiotics (stay out of the sun if on tetracyclines), birth control pills, aspirin and Tylenol®.

Be cautious about using seasick pills as they may cause drowsiness. If your physician prescribes a Transderm® Scop patch for seasickness, try it at home before diving to be sure that you are aware of any unde-sirable side effects.

Street drugs and alcohol do not mix with safe diving, nor does any mood-altering medication. All divers need to have their wits about them in order to safely handle any possible emergency situation. Such drugs can change your responses underwater, and can also increase your susceptibility to nitrogen narcosis and decompression sickness. The effect of many drugs remain in your body for days, and alcohol can be dangerous before, during and after diving.

WHAT ABOUT A COUGH?
IS IT OKAY TO DIVE WITH IT?

A cough represents chest congestion, and congestion is dangerous to a diver. Breathing compressed air mandates that we have healthy, clean and clear air passages. Any mucus in the lungs could block air passages, especially the tiny tubes. Air trapped in the air sacs (alveoli) behind the blockage will expand as we ascend, and could cause a lung over-expansion incident; you could suffer an air embolism! Even if your chest cold is weeks old, or your bronchitis attack was two months ago, if your cough persists, seek medical advice. Have yourself checked out before you go diving. Your lungs need to be clear. *Be careful.*

WHAT ABOUT SMOKING?

Smoking causes chest congestion. Smoke is an irritant and causes mucus production in the lungs while nicotine slows the body's natural mucus removal process. Therefore, it is dangerous to smoke, but even more dangerous for divers than for nondivers.

Smoking inhibits blood circulation and is implicated in the condi-tions predisposing us to DCS. Smoking also affects our physical fit-ness, and any diver who is not able to handle the physical requirements of diving is a danger to herself and to her buddy. There is no better time to stop smoking than now.

HOW FIT DO I NEED TO BE FOR DIVING?

"Sport diving is not usually a severe aerobic activity, so the differing capacity (between men and women, authors) for aerobic work should not matter," writes Dr. Tabby Stone, Medical Editor of *Discover Diving* Magazine. "It may, however, cause faster exhaustion when swimming against currents or performing heavy commercial work."[22]

So, everyone should stay in good shape. The best way to stay fit for diving is to dive frequently, but this is impractical for most of us. If you have a pool or ocean handy, vigorous fin-kicking with mask and snorkel is excellent conditioning. If this is unavailable for part or all of the year, almost any exercise will help.

Exercises that strengthen legs and provide cardiovascular conditioning, such as running, jogging, energetic walking, biking, basketball, etc., are excellent. Three sessions per week, of one-half hour or more, of sustained activity is about the minimum recommended for cardiovascular fitness. This schedule will keep you in shape for diving year-round.

I HAVE HAD SOME PLASTIC SURGERY. WILL I BE AFFECTED BY THIS WHILE DIVING?

Any surgery creates some amount of scar tissue. Divers are cautioned that scar tissue may not absorb and release nitrogen in the same manner as normal tissue. Theoretically, this means more susceptibility to DCS in the area. Usually, divers with scar tissue need to be more conservative in the use of the dive tables. Information suggests that the scar tissue from most plastic surgery is minimal and should cause no undue problems.

Nose surgery usually heals quickly and need not cause any distress. In fact, nasal passages may be in better shape for diving after nose surgery. Breast augmentation and reduction has not been shown to present problems. It is prudent to get medical clearance for diving following all surgeries.

OTHER MEDICAL CONDITIONS

While diving is safe for the vast majority of women pursuing this sport, there are some conditions under which it is not considered safe to dive.[13,23,24]

- Asthma
- Chronic obstructive/restrictive lung disease
- Lung cysts
- Spontaneous pneumothorax
- Chronic or severe problems of the ear
- Chronic or severe sinusitis
- Head injury with residual problems
- Epilepsy or other seizures
- Any heart or circulatory system condition which limits exercise, or is potentially uncontrollable or fatal
- Congenital heart disease with right-to-left shunting
- Insulin-dependent diabetes
- Certain anemias
- Certain mental or emotional illnesses

This partial list is in no way intended to be a final authority. Some conditions are not always apparent. Have a physical examination before embarking on your sport diving adventure and at regular intervals thereafter.

CHAPTER SEVEN

Managing Your Environment

"I was the only one in our group of four divers who bothered to take a compass bearing. We would have been hopelessly lost when the fog rolled in."

Jan Spak
Santa Monica, California

Your comfort level and safety as a diver increases right along with your skills. There is a tremendous amount to learn, though often divers feel that once they have mastered breathing from the regulator, they know how to dive. The greater your knowledge, the less you are dependent on physical strength. To that end, let's consider the following topics.

THE OCEAN

Learn as much as you can about the water in which you dive. This is especially true if you dive in the ocean, even though you may do so only on vacation. The ocean is considerably different than pools, small lakes, reservoirs, or quarries. Whatever else may be the case, it is salty, you are more buoyant, and it is always in motion. When you stand on the shore and look over the ocean, you can learn many things.

Bottom Type & Current

The shoreline is often indicative of the type of bottom. For example, a sandy shore most often means a sandy bottom. Know what to expect.

If there is a major current flowing just off shore, it is often visible from the land. You can sometimes tell by watching the movement of the ripples whether a current is flowing to the right or to the left. Also, if breaking waves are present and they meet the land at an angle, there will be a net movement in one direction along the shore. This is called a longshore current. Once you enter, you will be moved in the direction of the current. Plan ahead. Enter up current of your destination.

Surge

Waves in the ocean are created by the action of wind blowing for some distance across the surface of the water. Waves can travel great distances in the ocean. When the waves arrive at the shallower water near the shore, their effect can be felt underwater as surge. Surge is a back and forth movement of the water which can be disconcerting until you realize that it won't hurt you and can actually help you along in the direction you want to go. Relax. If you are moved laterally a few feet, you will be returned to your starting point.

Breakers

When waves reach the shore, they peak and break. Storms many miles away can create large local surf. While it is quite enjoyable to dive when the surf is small, diving during large surf is ill-advised. The conditions underwater will be poor. Go for a brisk walk on the beach instead. Remember, marginal surf can rapidly deteriorate to hazard-

*It is essential to learn as much as you can about the
local ocean before embarking on a dive.*

ous surf and even the idyllic resort areas can suffer poor conditions. (See section on shore diving later in this chapter.)

Sets and Lulls

Even when the conditions are good, the sizes of the breakers will vary. During a set, you may have several larger waves, say 3 or 4, followed by a lull during which you may have no waves or much smaller ones. Your ability to accurately distinguish the lull will add greatly to your comfort in diving from the shore. With your watch in hand, observe the breakers long enough to time several sets and lulls. Making marks in the sand to represent the relative size of each wave is an excellent way to record the wave size and the duration of the sets and lulls. Enter the water during the lull. If the lull is not long enough to enter safely, change to a more protected beach or have a picnic instead.

Tide

Tides are caused by the action of the sun and moon on the oceans. Some areas have a high tide and a low tide every day. Other areas have two each.

With practice it is a simple matter to determine wave sets and lulls.

It is often easier to enter and exit the water when the high tide covers obstructing rocks and plants.

High tide brings clean water in to shore and often allows easier access and increased visibility; you can float over rocks or aquatic plants instead of wading over them with your gear on. However, high tide also increases the size of the breaking waves in some areas.

Low tide may bring smaller surf but also lowered visibility . It may make shore entries more difficult in some areas.

In areas where large bays empty into the ocean, the tidal currents during the change from high to low (or vice versa) may be much too

101

strong for safe diving. You must time your dive to slack tide, a period of little or no currents.

Learn to read tide tables which tell you time and height of the tides. Also, ask local diving professionals for advice. Dive stores, lifeguards, and diving instructors are good sources of local information.

Visibility

Underwater visibility varies widely and is often caused by disturbed bottom sediments or by living organisms suspended in the water. Very poor visibility can cause stress and anxiety. However, diving in mid ocean with 200-foot visibility can also be disorienting. Most divers, even experienced ones, tend to underestimate underwater visibility, and reports of 5-foot visibility, when actually measured, turn out to be 10. Just because the visibility is low doesn't mean that you can't dive. Try shallow, quiet water at first. Use a 6-foot hand-held buddy line between you and your buddy. This should help reduce your anxiety about losing one another and give you the opportunity to observe things that you would otherwise miss, like tiny shrimp or fish. However, don't dive if you feel uncomfortable with the visibility.

Wind

Wind blowing across the lake or ocean will not only chill you between dives, but will create a choppy surface. In general, wind is greatest in the afternoon, and less in the early morning or at dusk. The wind will cause boats to swing back and forth and can be difficult to snorkel against, especially if your BC is fully inflated.

SHORE DIVING

In all diving, but especially so in shore diving, one of your major objectives should be to avoid overly stressing yourself, and to arrive at the dive site still capable of enjoying your dive. Because many persons find beach diving utterly exhausting, they assume that it is beyond

*With a little know-how, you can shore dive
without stress or strain.*

the level of their strength. However, you can compensate for lack of strength with planning, thinking, and improved skills.

Assemble your scuba gear and place your weight belt, mask, snorkel and fins within easy reach before undressing. By doing so you will conserve heat where the water or air temperature is chilly; where the sun is hot, you will prevent overheating. If you will be wearing a wetsuit, make all your observations, dive plans, and gear adjustments before getting into your suit. Dress into your suit slowly after everything else is ready. Avoid any standing around in all your gear. If you must walk while fully geared up, do so slowly. Don all your gear except your fins, complete a buddy check, and approach the water.

103

A buddy check consists of:

* Checking your buddy's pressure gauge;

* Checking the position of the reserve valve, if any;

* Acquainting yourself with the weight belt quick-release mechanism;

* Familiarizing yourself with the inflation device on the BC.

* Familiarizing yourself with your buddy's alternate air source and procedures for sharing.

If you are diving in very quiet water, proceed immediately into waist deep water, steady yourself with your buddy's help, put on your fins, and rest fully immersed. Then, shoulder to shoulder, snorkel to your dive site, stopping to rest at the first sign of breathlessness.

When surf is present, it is safest to don fins at the water's edge, but it is easier to walk into quiet water to put on your fins.

When entering through the surf, put on your fins with your buddy's help at the water's edge. Determine the beginning of the next lull, put your snorkel in position, face your buddy, and shuffle sideways or backwards into thigh deep water, and immediately lie down in a snorkeling position. If any breakers come along while shuffling out, lean toward the ocean, brace yourself with your legs, hold your mask in place with your seaward hand, and wait until the breaker passes. If you should fall, don't try to get up, but get into a snorkeling position as soon as possible.

When entering the water, brace yourself against breaking waves and rushing water.

From a snorkeling position, breakers look larger than they are. Don't get psyched out. A 2-foot breaker is still a 2-foot breaker. Start finning seaward with slow, strong kicks. Each time a breaker or white water approaches, keep your body at a right angle to the wave, take a deep breath, and make a shallow surface dive under the wave. Don't race. Monitor your breathing. If you are getting out of breath, stop where you are, face the ocean, breathe deeply, and make shallow surface dives when breakers approach. When you have caught your breath, continue kicking out.

When you dive beneath a breaker, you avoid the falling water which is moving shoreward. Don't wait for the breaker to reach you before starting your dive. Dive early; you'll be able to tell when the breaker passes overhead. You want your feet underwater when the breaker reaches you.

This technique works. Not convinced? Try it! Leave your scuba unit on the shore and enter with snorkeling gear only. Practice making those shallow surface dives until you feel at ease. Instead of watching an approaching breaker with dread, say to yourself, "I'm OK. I know what to do. I'll dive under it," then dive.

The distance you will have to travel to pass all the breakers is most likely shorter than the swimming pool you trained in. You can tell the distance before you leave the shore. When you arrive beyond the breaker zone, stop and rest. Then, shoulder to shoulder with your buddy, snorkel slowly to your dive site.

After your dive is over, stop just beyond the breaker zone opposite your exit point. Rest. While doing so, monitor the waves passing by and you will find that you can tell the sets from the lulls. Wait for a lull, then start snorkeling back to the shore. Use a right-side flutter kick, or kick toward the shore on your back. Watch the approaching waves. Should a large breaker approach, stop, reverse your direction of travel to head out toward the breaker, take a deep breath, and dive under it. Immediately resume kicking toward the shore. Repeat as needed.

Again, don't rush into breathlessness. If necessary, stop and rest, and use only as much energy as you need to dive under approaching waves. Shortness of breath in the surf leads rapidly to feelings of impending doom and panic.

When you arrive in water shallow enough for you to touch the bottom, don't try to stand. Hold your mask and let the smaller breakers push you towards the shore. Let the backwash (the water rushing back

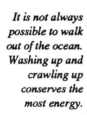

It is not always possible to walk out of the ocean. Washing up and crawling up conserves the most energy.

down the shore) pass under you, and crawl up the shore until you are completely out of the water. Rest. Then remove your fins, and get to your feet.

Make a conscious effort to conserve your energy throughout the entry, the dive, and the exit. As your skill in judging the conditions improves, you will find the dives taking less energy, and consequently, your enjoyment will grow.

BOAT DIVING

Divers who dislike boat diving are few indeed. I don't think I have ever met one. One of the main reasons is the ease of access to the dive site. Boat diving makes accessible the dive areas which you can't reach from shore. The entry is generally easy, a backward roll or giant stride, and an immediate descent without snorkeling any distance. Everyone loves it.

However, have you every heard horror stories of surfacing and the boat was a mere dot on the horizon, trying to snorkel back to the boat and not making progress, coming back to the boat underwater and every time you surface the boat is in a different place, and so on? What are the finer points that can help you master boat diving?

Always survey the prevailing conditions before going in for your dive.

Before suiting up, survey the conditions from the deck of the boat.

Current

Once the boat is at anchor, check by looking over the side for floating objects moving by, or aquatic plants leaning over. From the bow, look at the anchor line; is it making a small wake in the water? Look at the waterline at either side of the stern; is water swirling around the back of the boat? If the current is beyond your skill, you may want to sit out the dive. Remember, a current may exist only on or near the surface.

If you plan on going in, decide with your buddy to stay upcurrent of the boat and hold tenaciously to that plan. Currents are seductive, but unless the plan is for the divers and the boat to drift downstream, stay upcurrent. Pull yourself hand-over-hand along the line which sometimes extends from the entry gate to the anchor line. Then it's down the anchor line and into the current.

During a dive, be aware of the positions of plants, soft corals, and other current indicators. If they lean over, or you can feel the water movement, point out the change to your buddy, and while still on the bottom, move upcurrent of the boat before surfacing.

When there is a current, the crew will generally put out a current line to assist divers back to the boat. This line usually extends out from the back of the boat and has a float or flag on its end. Use it by swimming across the current to intersect the line between the boat and the end marker, then pull yourself hand over hand back to the boat. Save your energy and lower your anxiety!

Watch for signs of a current during the dive and dive upcurrent.

Wind

It is usually easy to tell if the wind is blowing, right? If it is, you have several things to consider. Wind chop will make snorkeling more difficult and will push against you if you are snorkeling upwind. Also, the wind will cause the boat to swing back and forth on the anchor line, unless the stern is anchored as well.

It is necessary to note the position of the boat prior to entering the water.

To exit the boat in the wind you and your buddy should enter the water without any delay between you. Your entry is best done when the boat is nearest the dive site to avoid unnecessarily long swims. Enter when the boat is moving away so you can descend without having the boat swinging on top of you.

Should you surface to take a bearing for returning underwater, aim your compass at the bow or the anchor line. These parts of the boat will change position less than the stern.

As you approach the stern to exit the water, remember that the boat will be moving back and forth. If you approach from the side while it is moving away, it may feel like you are swimming upstream in a strong current and you will never reach the boat. This is anxiety provoking and can cause great distress. Do remember that just as the boat swings away from you, it will swing back towards you. You can often maintain your position and merely wait for it to return.

NAVIGATION

It is not necessary nor is it much fun to blindly follow a buddy around. How do you find your way around on land? By noting landmarks, right? We do the same underwater. For instance, when you get to the bottom, there may be a large brain coral. You take note and then you go to the right past a cave with a lobster, continue on straight ahead to a tall pillar coral, then you decide it is time to turn around. All you need do is look for your landmarks, and when you arrive back at that brain coral, look up for the boat.

The use of the compass adds safety, confidence and efficiency to every dive. The buddy line ensures continuity of contact during poor visibility.

While we may trust our buddies to lead us back, don't do it because "I would be completely lost without him." You do more complicated maneuvering every day while finding your way through the streets.

Does the use of a compass completely befuddle you? Don't despair. It has some really simple functions. Some bare bones hints for many compasses are: simply hold the compass rigidly in front of you;

point the compass and your body in the direction you want to go; turn the bezel to mark the position of the floating needle; now descend and swim while keeping the floating needle matched to the marker on the bezel. Bingo, it works. You will arrive where you want to go. Practice it over and over, and believe in your compass. It won't get disoriented, even if you do.

Diving in kelp is a magical experience, but it requires a special orientation.

ENTANGLEMENTS

Even the thought of becoming entangled underwater can be frightening. The most important thing is to remain calm, continue to breathe and consider your alternatives.

Most aquatic plants can be broken by hand or bitten through if they can't be easily removed. Our biggest danger comes from man-made materials like rope and fishing line. Unfortunately, these occur more often than we'd like. Carry a small knife that is easily accessible to extricate yourself from those things than can't be broken by hand and from which neither you nor your buddy can disentangle you. It may be necessary to remove your tank and BC to clear unreachable entanglements. Keep yourself current in these skills by practicing in a pool.

SNORKELING IN SCUBA GEAR

Moving on the surface with scuba gear is certainly more difficult than without. Modify your expectation of progress. Settle for a slower pace and take your time.

It is important for all divers to be comfortable while resting or travelling on the surface.

Just being upright at the surface makes it harder to breathe. Your diaphragm is below your mouth. This slight difference in water pressure makes it harder to breathe. Try to reduce the amount of time you spend upright. Assume a horizontal position as quickly as possible and feel the immediate ease in breathing. Roll over and kick on your back if necessary.

113

Avoid over-inflating your buoyancy compensator. This greatly increases the effort required for you to move through the water. The large amount of air in the BC may also be putting pressure on your torso, making it harder to expand your chest and inhale. It is harder for you to get a breath, and that feels terrible. Remember, you didn't sink with just mask, snorkel and fins. A little air to support the tank and keep your snorkel above water, and away you go.

BUDDIES

If you are newly certified, you are justifiably proud of your C-card, and want to go diving, but you don't have a buddy. If none of your friends dive, how do you find someone with whom to dive? Start with your classmates. They often are in the same position, and you already know them.

Next, try dive clubs. Ask your instructor or your local dive store how to contact the clubs in your area. In metropolitan areas there will be several from which to choose. Some of these will cater to divers with special interests. There are photography clubs, hunting clubs, and general interest clubs, among others. In smaller communities there may be only one, so it will probably have members of varying interests. Go to club meetings and you'll meet a variety of people. Look for other women. Many may be having the same problem of locating dive partners.

How do you select a buddy? It is difficult for any diver, and more so for a female diver, as not everyone will accept you, your training, or your skills at face value. What do you do? Here are some suggestions.

Look first for divers with similar interests. If you hate the sight of dying fish, don't look among hunters for a buddy. Remember that many old salts (experienced divers) like to cruise around and look at things just like new divers. Tell them about yourself and ask about them. What do they like to do? What is their diving background? What is their air consumption like? If your first few conversations don't flush out an available buddy, don't get discouraged. Try again, and don't settle for one possibility. Cultivate several. Don't be shy about asking someone to buddy up. It could be the beginning of a wonderful friendship.

Go on club or other group dives alone and ask the dive-master to help you round up other single divers. Take the time to become acquainted and ask the above questions. Include others like: When was your last dive? Do you buddy breathe or use the safe 2nd stage only?

Buddies do well to take into consideration common air consumption, pacing, interests and repetitive dive-letter groups.

How do you handle an out-of-air emergency? What is your hand signal for "I'm cold and want to go back?" How do you signal you are "low on air?" When you decide to dive together, don't get in the water until you have a definite dive plan: maximum depth, direction, objective, turn-around psi, emergency plans, signs, etc. Then do a buddy check: amount of air, how BC inflators work, how weight belts work.

Does this seem like a lot of work? It isn't really, and you'll meet others in the same position who will appreciate your taking the initiative. Diving with a stranger or a new buddy needs careful planning.

Don't pass it by for fear of offending. You will gain more respect for your own abilities, and you will avoid nightmare experiences with buddies who have a totally different idea of what the dive is to be like.

MISCELLANY

You are on a small boat without a head (toilet), and you have been correctly forcing fluids all morning. Do you sit there and squirm, or do you go in snorkeling? Snorkeling, of course. Just ignore all those hydrodynamically equipped males as they stand casually facing the stern of the boat.

Many women dive even during heavy menstrual flow. The only problems associated with this are ones of convenience. Bring lots of tampons for frequent changes as the tampon absorbs water while diving. When it is saturated it is no longer effective.

If there are no fresh-water showers available, and it is hot and humid, must you endure being sticky for hours after your dive? Not necessarily. Dry the salt water off with a towel immediately, wipe with a fresh-water moistened cloth, then dry off again.

If your hair is a sticky fuzzball, break out the salt-water shampoo which you had the foresight to bring and watch the envious stares. But don't dump your suds into the ocean. If you take a bath in the ocean, use only biodegradable soap.

SAFETY

Your diving safety depends on yourself. The major cause of diving accidents is panic. Eliminate as many factors that would cause you to panic as possible. *There is always an excellent alternative to a panicked response.* All you have to do is put it into action.

- Plan your dives: where, when (day, night, high tide, etc.), with whom, and how.

- Communicate: hand signals, light signals, written communications, etc.

- Have sound diving equipment: keep everything in good repair with regular service and inspections whether you are diving or not.

- Master proper weighting and buoyancy control techniques.

- Practice good buddy diving techniques: side by side, not "follow the leader."

- Review emergency procedures: keep current by practicing air sharing in a safe area with an agreeable buddy.

- Review rescue procedures: self-rescue is as important as buddy-rescue.

- Get refresher or continuing training: we all have lots more to learn.

- Read! This is a sport in its infancy and new information is being continuously published. This new information could be vital to your health, well-being and enjoyment. Keep in touch.

- Enlarge your practical diving knowledge to increase your diving pleasure and your safety.

CHAPTER EIGHT

The Emotional You

"The surf was very big that day and we were all scared, but the women were the first to bring it out in the open and question the wisdom of the dive."

Jean Hawkins, M.D.
Dive Instructor

Women are generally regarded as being emotional. As a diver, your emotionality can enhance your enjoyment of diving. You can find great joy in being weightless, in the translucent delicacy of an orange-ball anemone, or in the grandeur of the kelp forest.

Some people regard women as too emotional for diving. Perhaps they are referring to our willingness to cry. If something goes awry and one gets upset, then obviously she must be an overly emotional person. Don't let this stereotype hamper your progress in diving. An angry man is not often referred to as being too emotional. So, if you get clobbered by a wave and, in the aftermath, tears come to your eyes, so what? Please, don't consider that you are less a diver because of those tears! Being emotional can often be an asset instead of a hindrance.

What about fear? Does making a night dive give you the heebie-jeebies? We are all beset by fear of the unknown, fear of the dark, fear of things that "go bump in the night." Once successfully experienced, the trepidation disappears.

Do you remember the first time you put on a pair of roller skates, ice skates, or skis? What was your greatest fear? Falling and/or hurting yourself, right? Perhaps being out of control? As you gained skill and confidence, the fear subsided, and you soon found that in most instances you could control being afraid. Diving plugs into even more elemental fears: the dark; not being able to breathe; known and un-

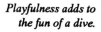

*Playfulness adds to
the fun of a dive.*

known monsters, etc. These fears produce stress in all divers, and your response to this stress depends on a lot of factors.

As you can tell by observation, some people are more anxious than others. Individuals with a naturally high level of anxiety usually don't take up diving, or they may drop out before completing the class. Some special individuals have found that persevering and working through their fears have given them not only a new sport to enjoy, but a new outlook on life.

But we all have some background level of anxiety, as well as certain circumstances which scare us silly. Don't for a moment think that you are the only one experiencing a particular fear. Take heart and speak up. Tell your buddy or dive leader your concerns. Fortunately, women are usually good about verbalizing their fears. This factor alone is a great advantage to you in diving.

HOW CAN YOU MANAGE YOUR FEARS AND STILL DIVE?

Become a well-trained, highly skilled, and non-dependent diver.

As discussed in Chapter 2, shop for the best possible training for yourself and plan on becoming the most highly skilled diver that you can. Realize that scuba skills take practice, and with practice you will become more proficient. None of the diving techniques are impossible, and your goal of becoming an independent diver is within your reach.

Take additional courses as necessary for you to become a highly-skilled diver.

The thought of water in your mask unnerves you? You have difficulty getting down? Unsure about underwater navigation? Seek additional training. You become so exhausted after the second dive that you have to be pulled onto the boat? Start a program to improve your physical strength and fitness.

Do you dive only with your boyfriend because he takes care of all the equipment, dive planning, and leading the dive? You and your boyfriend are both in danger. It is unsafe to be a dependent diver. Seek the training necessary to master the basic skills: caring for equipment, planning a dive, following a compass course, leading a dive, and assisting or rescuing a buddy. (To learn more about self-sufficiency, refer to the book "Solo Diving: The Art of Underwater Self-Sufficiency" by Robert von Maier.)

Take an active part in planning all your dives.

Regardless of your size, weight, or strength, you are in control of your destiny as a diver. Learn to plan within your abilities and endurance. Learn how to assess the water conditions and decide when not to dive. You arrive at the water's edge and look around. A strong current is running. Express yourself clearly and specifically. "The current is too strong for me. Let's wait a while until it slackens." Don't let yourself be talked into it and enter the water in an uncomfortable state.

Take your turn in leading the dive and assume some of the responsibility for controlling the dive.

Plan on leading and making the decisions for at least half the dive. During your pre-dive discussion, just say something like, "I'll lead the way out, and you lead the way back". Leading doesn't mean being out in front leaving your buddy to stare at your fins. It means being shoulder to shoulder, but taking the responsibility of indicating places to stop and places to go. Learn to communicate with more sophisticated hand signals so you can clarify leadership underwater, among other things. A buddy team is a partnership. If one buddy is acting "leader," he/she is probably running the compass course. It falls to the other buddy to maintain proper depth and monitor air supplies. "Follower" is not an unimportant role.

During the dive, don't hesitate to communicate your needs to your buddy. Say or write, "We're too deep. Let's go up." Or "I'm too cold.

You will have a far better time underwater if you lead your share of the dives.

Let's go back." Your welfare and comfort are just as important as your buddy's, although as women we sometimes put ourselves last. So often we have heard women say, "I was uncomfortable, but I didn't want to spoil it for my buddy." Keep in mind that no matter how generous you may feel, it is unsafe to dive while miserable. Any worthwhile buddy or dive leader should react to your comments or concerns in a calm, reasonable and non-judgmental way. Find a dive partner who is sensitive to your needs or one who gets cold when you do.

As your unfounded fears decrease, you will learn more and progress even more rapidly in your diving skills. Needless to say, you will enjoy yourself more. However, the unexpected will happen. This often creates stress and generates the stress responses. Your heart pounds, your rate of breathing increases, you sweat, and your muscles tense. If unchecked, this can lead to panting, shortness of breath, and fatigue or exhaustion. These responses create seemingly insurmountable feelings of inadequacy, helplessness, and doom, which in turn make the heart pound, starting the vicious cycle over again. You **must** break the cycle before it leads to full-blown panic.

Diving is a sport enjoyed by thousands of couples and families.

As soon as you are aware of growing stress, STOP whatever you are doing; BREATHE with deep inhalations and long, full exhalations; THINK about what is happening and what you can do; then ACT.

Example: You are diving in the Caribbean and follow the divemaster/guide into a coral passageway with your group. The diver ahead of you kicks up the sand and you can see nothing. Your heart pounds and you feel that you are suffocating. STOP moving, BREATHE long full breaths, THINK "I can breathe, I have plenty of air, I'm OK, the sand will settle down in a few minutes," then ACT by moving forward slowly with an outstretched hand until you are out of the sand cloud. You can also rise-up slightly over the sand cloud to where the visibility is OK to regain orientation or find your buddy.

Example: You and your buddy are both entranced by a sea lion. You don't notice that you are on her heels, and she doesn't notice that she has just kicked off your mask. Well, you don't need a mask to breathe, do you? Stay calm, open your eyes and look for that mask. It must be near. Sure enough, it is within the reach of your hand. You put it back on, clear it of water and the only discomfort you have suffered is the surprise of the cold water on your face. Your buddy never even noticed, and she is embarrassed you were able to manage all that without her being aware you were in any trouble!

Your creativity can enhance your diving activities.

Fear must be held back long enough for your training to take effect. Your body's response will actually change your perception of the situation until it is all out of proportion. Suddenly, the 6-inch wind chop is as threatening as 6-foot waves.

If there is some particular circumstance which gives you a lot of trouble, you can reduce the anxiety associated with it by mentally rehearsing the experience to a successful conclusion several times. Every aspect of diving that you conquer makes you a better, safer diver.

Let's say you went on a beach dive and got tumbled in the surf. Try to avoid getting locked into a fixed "I-hate-beach-diving" position. The following week, the surf could be ankle-high! Instead, improve your skill in assessing the conditions to determine what you can handle, and go diving during the periods when you can enjoy yourself.

Do you sometimes feel intimidated by the diving tales you hear? Often the storytellers are loud, talkative divers who exude confidence and invincibility. Ignore them. Most of these stories contain vast exaggerations. In any case, the macho diver who ran out of air in a lava tube and had to swim 100 feet horizontally before making a 90-foot emergency swimming ascent should not be admired; they had no business running out of air. It is totally unnecessary and extremely careless.

You can easily avoid all persons who belittle you for your apprehensions. Find someone else with whom to train and/or dive. Women bring something special to the world of diving; something unforeseen when it all began. We have every reason to feel competent and accomplished in our chosen sport. Believe in yourself and your special gifts.

When Women Dive

CHAPTER NINE

When You Travel

*"My style of travel has certainly changed.
Now I look for diving everywhere I go."*

Nancy Adams
Forestville, Maryland

Actually, all of our diving involves some travel, doesn't it? It may be travel by auto or boat involving less than a half hour or travel by plane for many hours. It may be travel we do on a frequent basis or the trip of a lifetime. There are some considerations that can make traveling more pleasurable for you.

A DIVING TRIP OR A TRIP WITH DIVING?

Some of us go to the tropical isles primarily to dive, and othersgo for the luscious locale for the sun, sand, fun and just a little diving. This is an important differentiation to make at the time you are first planning your trip. If you want to dive, make certain diving is available. Do not take it for granted.

If you are mainly interested in diving, you have some investigating to do. Dive travel is a specialty unlike any other form of travel. The destinations vary widely. Indeed, there is excellent diving in every ocean of the world. Since divers spend so much time on and under the water, accommodations seem to be of less importance. Many divers are content with good food and clean rooms, leaving the rest of the travel budget for the diving and traveling expenses. This does not mean that many dive resorts do not have lovely accommodations and a great atmosphere.

Dive resorts are very different from other types of resorts. The principal concern is the ways and means of diving. The diving establishment intends your dive to be easy, hassle-free and as great as they can make it. They know you were attracted there by the diving. This type of resort may be off the beaten path. It exists there because the underwater world is better there.

Resort hotels on the other hand, may or may not have diving facilities. You may have to contract with an outside business to take you diving. These arrangements may or may not be simple, and it is almost always more expensive to dive independently on a day-to-day basis than in a package through a "diving resort". If you are not going to dive often, and prefer the ambience of a resort hotel, then it may not be of great concern to you.

If your focus is on diving, it is usually simpler to arrange for a prepaid dive plan that includes everything. You probably won't have to haul gear around, the boat will be docked nearby, the times will be arranged conveniently for the majority of divers, and the underwater scenery will be fantastic. This takes most of the work out of your diving vacation.

It is much less expensive per dive when you purchase a prepaid dive package. However, if you decide to go this route, you should ask some pertinent questions:

1. How many days of diving are included?
2. How many dives per day are included?
3. What time of day are the dives?
4. Are these boat dives or beach dives?
5. Are any night or other special dives included?
6. What equipment is included?

LIVE-ABOARD BOATS

Although live-aboard boats have long been available around the world, they are becoming more numerous each year. There is much to be said for a vacation on a live-aboard dive boat, but it is definitely a dive vacation, not a vacation with diving. If you are not a scuba diver, you will probably not be happy for a week or so on a live-aboard. Liveaboards should not be confused with cruise ships that have lots of other activities.

Live-aboard boats will average between 50 to 125 feet (15 to 38 meters) long, and will accommodate somewhere between four and forty divers plus crew.

The accommodations may be luxurious or may be barely adequate. However as divers are becoming more demanding as to the quality of their housing, more and more boats are becoming available in the luxury category.

All diving involves travel to some extent.

Live-aboard dive boats have become very popular.
They provide easy access to sites and virtually
unlimited diving.

Liveaboards are certainly the way to maximize your diving and open diving up to many excellent locations that are only accessible by a live-aboard dive boat. Many parts of the Great Barrier Reef and the Coral Sea, for example, are too far from the mainland to be dived any other way.

There is usually unlimited diving from a live-aboard, but ask in advance. It is wonderful to be able to jump into the water before breakfast, and virtually any other time you want. This kind of freedom attracts serious divers to the many charter live-aboard vessels found around the world. You cannot find easier diving anywhere.

EQUIPMENT, IN GENERAL

It is much more desirable to dive with your own than with rental equipment. If you own any of your own equipment, TAKE IT WITH YOU. Take as much as you have or can. The hassle of packing and transporting diving equipment is small compared to the inconvenience and considerable cost associated with rentals.

Snorkeling and skin-diving add hours of enjoyment to your trip.

MASK, SNORKEL, FINS, GLOVES AND BOOTIES

Masks and snorkels have improved so much in fit, comfort and attractiveness in recent years that you will want to have your own. Masks and snorkels in rental are often limited in styles and sizes. So, at the very least, take your own mask, snorkel, fins, gloves and booties. (See Chapter 5 on gloves.)

Once you have your own equipment, you will no longer be happy with the choices available in rental gear. If not previously purchased, now is the time to do so. Money spent renting gear would be better put toward purchasing your own. Then you will be free to go snorkeling or skin diving whenever and wherever you want, in your own comfortable equipment. If you only intend to dive occassionaly, this is the minimum amount of equipment you will need to purchase.

REGULATOR AND GAUGES

If you have your own regulator and gauges, take them. Pack your regulator and gauges carefully, and pad them as you would any sensitive equipment. If you are flying, protect all gauges sensitive to pressure, such as depth gauges and timers, from radical pressure changes.

Otherwise, their accuracy may be affected. One way to protect them is to pack them in the airtight boxes available at the dive equipment store, and check them through with the rest of your dive gear. Or, especially for sensitive equipment like dive computers, carry them aboard with you in your hand luggage. Remember in the pressure in the passenger compartment is the same as in the luggage compartment. So, if needed, an airtight box is required whether you check or carry your sensitive equipment with you.

If you do not own your own regulator and gauges, phone ahead to your dive destination and inquire as to the types of regulators and gauges they carry. You may find that they do not rent equipment with which you would be happy. Or you may find the only gauges they rent are submersible pressure gauges. Even if you intend to go only on supervised dives, it is absolutely necessary for each diver (YOU) to have a depth gauge and underwater timing device on their person. It is not unimaginable or unheard of for you to become separated from the guide or to dive deeper that your leader and/or your buddy. This may be accidental or intentional, but you must know how deep you've gone and how long you've stayed. You may not be able to rely on another diver, even if you wanted to. So, it may be necessary for you to purchase gauges prior to your diving trip.

A compass may or may not be necessary, depending on circumstances.

NOTE: To avoid equipment problems during your trip, have your regulator and gauges serviced before you depart especially if they haven't been serviced within the last year. The repair center will check the gauges, hoses, O-rings, etc. This minimizes the chance of having a leaky pressure gauge or a hose rupture on your trip.

BUOYANCY COMPENSATORS

Since most women are normally buoyant in salt water, snorkelers and skin divers do not necessarily need a buoyancy compensator. However to make the activity more comfortable or as a resting station on the surface, a skin diving vest may be utilized. It is not as large as a scuba BC, but has adequate lifting ability to increase your comfort. A few breaths of air in your vest will keep you happily afloat.

Again, you will enjoy having all your own vest or BC. Rental BC's may not come in a wide selection of sizes, and smaller people in particular should take their own. Also, rental BC's may be more or less padded than those to which you are accustomed, so you may not be as comfortable and you may need to weight yourself differently.

The rental BC's may be of an unfamiliar style. There are many BC models. The horse collar variety goes over your head, around your

The numerous West Coast dive boats play host to thousands of divers each year.

neck and requires the use of a crotch strap to hold it in place and a separate backpack to hold your tank. One French-made BC requires hook-
ing the restraining strap to your weight belt, making the weight belt
more difficult to remove in a hurry. Do not take for granted that you
are going to be able to dive contentedly with just any BC that will be
available. Find out ahead of time just what you will be using.

While still on the subject of BC's, don't forget that the power inflator fitting on a rental BC must match the power inflator hose fitting
on your regulator.

TANKS, WEIGHTS AND BELTS

Generally speaking, if you are flying, don't bother taking your
tank. Most dive resorts include tanks in your dive package. In some
remote places it is impossible to rent a tank, and even if you had one,
you probably couldn't get it filled. Any location that has a high percentage of divers coming from out of town will probably provide tanks
and weights.

One notable exception to the above rule is some of the U.S. and the
Canadian west coast. The vast majority of divers utilizing these dive
facilities come from near by, generally within driving range. Therefore, the diving industry hasn't fully geared up to provide tanks and
weights.

The prime destination for most traveling divers coming to the west
coast of the United States is the dozens of charter dive boats that spend
from one day to a week diving the thousands of miles of shore line and
the many islands just off shore. Probably close to half will have tanks
and weights on board for you, but that means half will not. If the boat
does not provide tanks, you can bring your own, or rent from one of the
many convenient dive shops in nearby cities. Call ahead to ask what is
included in the cost of diving, and the price of those things which are
extra.

NOTE: Tanks must be completely empty to be transported on planes and helicopters.

No one carries lead weights on commercial flights. Lead inside your gear bag makes it difficult to carry, will ruin your dive bag, will crush your and other people's gear, and the airline may charge you for overweight. It is just easier to rent weights there. Not every operation that rents weights provides the belts. Don't take this for granted. ASK. In any case, belts without the weights are easy to take.

Women in particular find it more convenient to bring their own belt, and thread it with the resort's weights. Most rental belts are 50 inches (1.25 meters) long to accommodate *everyone*. You won't want all that excess webbing hanging out making you unsafe (and looking dorky). If you must use such a long belt, remember to fold the excess back under the buckle.

Take your own weight stays to keep the lead from sliding around and getting into uncomfortable places.

NOTE: The one exception we make to traveling with weights is our 3-pound ankle weights. So far, they are not available for rental anywhere.

Left to right: 1/4" jacket over a Lycra suit; 1/8" full wetsuit; 1/4" jacket over dance tights; 1/8" body with 1/16" sleeves.

Women are generally more comfortable in some form of wetsuit, like this shorty, even in warm water.

WETSUITS

Most of us are more comfortable on an extended dive vacation with some thermal protection. Do you plan on one dive a day, or two, or three, plus a night dive? As discussed in Chapter 5, if you plan to do more than one or two dives a day, you will enjoy yourself more if you wear some thermal protection. Find out the average water temperature of your destination, and with the help of Table 5.2 in Chapter 5, plan your needs. Many common dive destinations (Hawaii, the Bahamas,

Australia) have water temperatures low enough to need protection. Besides, it's easier to handle being a little too warm underwater than being too cold.

Warmer waters of 75° F (25° C) and above.

For frequent exposure, the 1/8 or 3/16 inch (3 or 5 mm) full-length one piece wetsuit is recommended. If you are you planning to snorkel, skin dive, or only make one scuba dive per day, then a "shorty" (short arms and legs) will probably suffice. You can often rent a shorty. If you intend to purchase your own suit, shop surfing stores in addition to dive stores.

If you already own a full 1/4 inch (7 mm) suit, either the jacket or the farmer john alone may be just what you need for your warm water trip. If you use the jacket alone, a lycra suit or leg tights worn beneath the jacket will protect your legs from the "stingies."

Colder water of 55° to 75° F (13° to 25° C).

Rental suits are much more common in colder water areas because local divers rent suits also. Call ahead, determine the thickness and conformation of rental suits, and reserve one. If the water is colder than 65° F (18° C), you will be uncomfortable in anything less than 1/4 inch (7 mm) suit complete with a jacket, farmer john, hood and gloves.

DRYSUITS

Drysuit rentals are becoming much more common in cold water areas. If you are planning a dive vacation to a cold water area and you are not a regular drysuit user, get instruction and practice in their use before you leave home.

MAINTAINING EQUIPMENT

You will have fewer problems both during and after your vacation if you are able to rinse your gear with fresh water as often as possible. Boats do not generally carry enough fresh water to rinse any but the most expensive equipment (cameras, computers), but most resorts are aware of this need and provide fresh water rinsing stations.

ACCESSORIES

Don't forget to pack your dive light. Just because you may be traveling to an area where the water is clear doesn't mean you won't want to explore nooks and crannies, see color underwater, and night dive. Lights add color and a lot of pleasure to diving, and they are not often available for rental.

If you are traveling abroad, check on the electrical voltage and amperage available. This is important if you plan to charge batteries for lights, strobes, or power packs of any kind. You may use voltage converters and adaptors, or travel with alkaline batteries to keep it simple. Remember, however, that batteries and film are much more expensive in resort areas and that batteries may be a limited commodity.

In some areas with difficult power problems, the dive and photo facilities may have charging stations available to protect your valuable equipment. Check it out.

GEAR BAG

The size of the bag you need for your diving gear will depend on how much you own and what you take with you. However much it is, you need a bag to keep your equipment together and organized. If you are taking only snorkeling gear, you may be able to add it to your clothing bag, but you will still enjoy having a small bag in which to carry it once you get there. If you take all the equipment necessary to scuba dive, you will need a bag dedicated to gear.

A well constructed bag of sturdy material will serve you best, especially if flying to a dive destination is included in your plans. Your expensive dive gear is best protected from rough and ready baggage handlers by a good bag and adequate padding.

*Your dive vacation is enhanced by photographs, but packing
camera gear demands more precise planning.*

Unfortunately, as dive equipment has gone up in price, so has the
rate of thefts from airports. In this case, it doesn't pay to advertise! If
you are shopping for a bag, don't opt for the one that shouts, "Pick me
to steal – I've got expensive diving equipment inside!" Rather, choose
a bag without a diving manufacturer's name on it. Your gear is safer
when it travels incognito. It is heartbreaking to arrive at your destination without your gear bag, and this happens all too often.

PACKING

Divers must become good packers. We haul around so many more
things than the average traveler that we need to give a lot more thought
to how we pack for a trip.

How many bags do you need to take? It is not a good idea to take
just one bag. If that one is lost, not only is your dive gear missing, but

your clothes as well. It's too catastrophic to even contemplate. Some divers divide two bags equally; both contain some clothes and some equipment. The rationale is if one is lost, they still have some clothes and some gear. Once both bags safely arrive, they can be repacked into separate bags for convenience. This makes a lot of sense. This combination also allows for the clothing to be utilized as packing material for the more delicate equipment, cutting down on the overall bulk and weight of each bag. Remember, two light bags are much easier for women to handle than one heavy bag.

Baggage allowance varies from airline to airline; some airlines serving prime dive areas even allow dive gear to go free, so be sure to inquire. It is best to know in advance how much you are allowed, including carry-ons.

The opportunity to visit famous wrecks is but one of the things that make dive travel so exciting.

Always pack your sweatsuit and your tennis shoes.

Pack as if gorillas will be stomping on your fragile paraphernalia. Breakables such as your mask, regulator, and gauges must be protected with padding. A wetsuit works well, if you are packing one. A padded BC may also work well.

Do not take a chance on losing a particularly valuable piece of gear, especially those components that are not usually available for rental. We recommend you hand carry a dive computer as well as your gauge console. The loss of these items may make it difficult for you to dive safely.

Be sure to take your C-card, dive tables and your log book. Some resorts ask to see your dive log to verify diving experience, and all require your certification card.

CARRY-ON LUGGAGE

Although the airline industry has tightened up on hand carried luggage, it is prudent to carry as much as you can. Luggage is often delayed, if not lost, and we have envied well organized women who have tucked a bathing suit, a change of lingerie and a spare T-shirt into their carryall. If you use a prescription mask, include that as well.

The traveling diver makes many new friends.

Take a lightweight sweater or jacket for those long, icy hours in an air-conditioned plane. If it is going to be a trip of some duration, you will relish the opportunity to freshen up. Include a small supply of personal items like toothbrush, toothpaste, astringent, lotion, etc. You will know best what should be on your personal list.

Juggling all these bags can be difficult if you also need to hand carry such items as photographic gear. It can be managed, however, by not carrying a handbag. Include a small, collapsible handbag in your carryall, and consider your carryall as your handbag. Just make certain it is not so large that it looks like luggage and be absolutely sure it will fit under a seat.

LUGGAGE INSURANCE

Generally speaking, airline insurance allows a maximum payment of about $600 per lost bag. This does not begin to cover the loss of a bag full of diving equipment. Also, airline insurance may not cover a loss if you check your bag at the curb. Consider other options such as your homeowners or household insurance policies, credit card, and other insurance companies. Check to be sure, but they often cover a casualty loss that occurs when traveling. Some credit card companies, like American Express, provide additional coverage for lost baggage if the airline tickets are charged on their card. **WARNING:** Photographic and sporting equipment is often exempt from this coverage, so read the fine print.

HUNTING LICENSE

If you are a hunter, keep in mind that many warm water resort areas do not allow any hunting by tourists. They want to protect the marine life and the environment for future travelers. Other areas have local fish and game laws, most of which require a fishing license. If you hunt in any area, make certain you know the local laws and the locations of game preserves.

SPARE PARTS

Carrying a spare mask strap, a couple of spare fin straps, tank and regulator O-rings, snorkel keeper, and a small tool kit for your equipment in a small, waterproof box could save a dive and your entire vacation. It's an easy way to avoid hassles and disappointments.

INOCULATIONS

See your physician for any recommended inoculations for your destination(s).

FIRST AID KIT

Unfortunately, you cannot rely on the availability of appropriate first aid materials on dive boats or even back at the hotel or lodge. It is prudent to carry your own basics, and very wise to carry the items that pertain to diving injuries. The following is a suggested list for a minimal first aid kit. Again, it is ideal to carry the contents in a small, waterproof box since it should always be with your dive gear.

FIRST AID KIT CONTENTS

Aspirin
Motion sickness medication
Bandaids®
Bandages
Waterproof tape
Neosporin® or other antibacterial ointment
Polysporin® powder (by prescription)
Vinegar
Hydrogen peroxide
Insect repellent
Sun block and/or suntan lotion
Eye drops
Ear drops
Antibacterial anesthetic ointment/cream
Cortisone cream
A general oral antibiotic for infections, etc.

VENOMOUS MARINE LIFE

It is your responsibility to educate yourself as to the potentially dangerous marine life in each locale. There are marine organisms which can cause discomfort. Sponges can be poisonous, as can worms, corals, hydroids, starfish, sea wasps, jellyfish, and some fish. The sting of some of these creatures can be merely uncomfortable for a short time. Others cause greater discomfort for a longer period of time. In a few cases, the sting can be fatal. For instance, in some waters there are shells that are deadly (actually the snails that live in the shells). Some people are much more sensitive to these stings than others, just as some people are very allergic to poison ivy or bee stings while others are not.

Rather than find out the hard way, learn what to leave alone. You will enjoy your dives a great deal more when you know what you can touch and what you must avoid.

While some marine life stings are of little consequence and others are quite uncomfortable, you will profit by being prepared to deal with

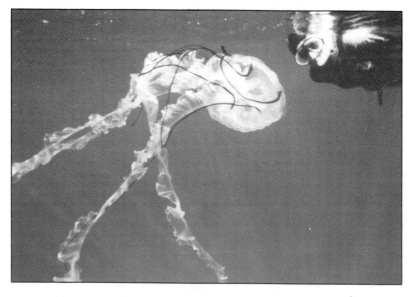

It is vital that you familiarize yourself with all forms of marine life.

any malady by knowing the appropriate first aid treatment. A list of the most common stings and the first aid treatment follows:

- **Coral cuts and scrapes:** *Wash thoroughly with a mild soap and apply Polysporin® powder.*
- **Fire Coral stings:** *Apply vinegar or meat tenderizer.*
- **Fire Sponge stings:** *Remove spicules with adhesive tape and apply cortisone cream.*
- **Fire Worm stings:** *Remove bristles with adhesive tape and apply cortisone cream.*
- **Jellyfish stings:** *Remove tentacles and apply vinegar.*
- **Sea Wasp stings:** *Apply vinegar.*
- **Crown of Thorns stings:** *Remove barb, apply heat and seek medical attention.*
- **Hydroid stings:** *Apply vinegar.*
- **Stingray stings:** *Apply heat and seek medical attention.*
- **Sea Urchin spine punctures:** *Remove spine and apply hydrogen peroxide to the wound; if any spine remains, apply heat to the wound.*
- **Scorpionfish and Stonefish:** *Apply heat and seek medical attention.*
- **Lionfish, Zebrafish, etc.:** *Apply heat and seek medical attention.*

IN THE EVENT OF A DIVE ACCIDENT OR ILLNESS

If you feel you are suffering from a dive related illness and you need advice as to symptoms, treatment, transportation, etc., telephone the **DIVER ALERT NETWORK**, known among divers as **DAN**. They are located at Duke University, Durham, North Carolina, U.S.A. and provide a 24-hour Diving Medical Assistance number: **(919) 684-8111**.

This telephone number should be kept permanently with your dive gear. The non-emergency Medical and Safety Advice number is (919) 684-2948 and is open during business hours.

DAN is a private, diver-supported network. The membership fee is quite reasonable. In addition, health insurance for dive accidents is available to current members. The annual premium is inexpensive.

HEALTH/DIVE ACCIDENT INSURANCE

As some divers have unhappily discovered, all health insurance policies do not cover dive related accidents and illnesses. In addition to DAN, there are several companies offering dive accident insurance. Many health insurance policies do not cover the often expensive transportation costs. If hyperbaric treatment is required, your ambulance may have to be a helicopter, or a private, low flying airplane. There is not always a chamber nearby; in fact, it may be located some distance away. For example, there is currently a chamber on the island of Grand Cayman, and there is one on the island of Bonaire, but the nearest recompression chamber to Belize and Roatan is in Panama! At present, there are none in Tahiti, and it's a long way to Hawaii. Always be extremely conservative in your diving.

We've found that divers don't spend that much time off the water. We always bring too many clothes, and invariably return home with a few clean (never worn) clothes. These garments run the gamut from "dressier" to casual. There will be at lease once when you are too tired to make it to dinner (pack one less outfit). You will go to breakfast in your bathing suit at least once, and you will sleep in at least once (two less "breakfast" outfits). Lunch is casual, and you know you are going to buy at least one set of "things," so pack another outfit less. (No matter how many oaths you swear, you will but a T-shirt or two.)

There are a lot of benefits to spending so much time in the water. Divers need to take fewer clothes than the average "what in the world are we going to do now" tourists. We don't need to take tennis outfits, biking outfits, golfing outfits, shopping outfits, and sight-seeing outfits. However, unless you are totally knocked out every night, you will have to pack a few party clothes. For divers this often means anything you feel good in. Dive resorts are casual, and you will stand out in white

Beach shoes are a must.

pants, T-shirt and your tan!. Your sarong can be tied in a dozen different ways, and you will glow in the aftermath of perfect days of diving.

An integral part of your dive gear should be a waterproof windbreaker. Available at nominal cost at your local sporting goods store
in sets with jacket and pants, these items will greatly increase your
enjoyment by reducing the wind chill factor. Between dives, cover up
your wetsuit or swimsuit, unless you are in a really warm environment.
The evaporation of water removes a lot of heat from your body, something that you can ill afford unless you are diving in water close to your
body temperature. Diving areas with water temperatures of 90° F (32°
C) and above are uncommon.

In cooler areas, add a woolen cap and gloves. Hoard every last fraction of a degree of body heat, and replace lost heat between dives with hot drinks.

You know those fancy swimsuits with buttons, bows, strings or trim? They are a royal pain under a wetsuit. Stick with plain undecorated maillots, and save the fancies for the beach and those swim parties.

The full length lycra suits are wonderful — alone for some protection in warm water and under wetsuits in cooler waters. However, they will chill you quickly because of evaporative cooling. Cover up when above water. The newest versions have a windproof barrier so that this cooling does not occur.

Did you know that fabric softeners can help tame that stiff wetsuit? You will find improved flexibility.

Flip Flops! How did we ever get along without them? Actually, beach shoes don't need to be flip flops, but you'll want some type of waterproof sandal. You'll use them for everything from beach walking, coral protection, hot sidewalks, rocky beaches, rinsing gear, etc.

NOTE: No matter what the climate, you can never predict the weather, especially on the water. Always go prepared. Even the Caribbean in January can be cold! I know you are not planning for your dive days to be ruined by rain and wind, but it does happen doesn't it? Don't go ANYWHERE without a couple of sweatshirts and a windbreaker as the minimum (unless you are going to but "Dive the Bahamas" sweatshirts there). Some of the more luxurious live-aboard dive boats in the tropics keep their salons and staterooms too air-conditioned for our comfort. We need our sweats.

VACATION INSURANCE

In this day of prepaid airline tickets and prepaid dive vacations, it is scary to consider losing a healthy deposit or even your entire investment in case of illness or other complications. Vacation or trip insurance can provide the means to have protection and still take advantage

Dive travel provides many special moments.

of the prepayment packages. An application can be obtained through your travel agent. Read the fine print as to exactly what cancellation circumstances are covered by the policy.

STAYING HEALTHY

Here are some considerations when you are diving during a trip.

1. We are more disposed to decompression sickness when we are tired, out-of-shape, and hung-over.

2. Drinking, drugs and diving don't mix, so don't be tempted to dive if you're under the influence of either.

3. There is evidence to suggest that it may take longer than twelve hours to clear our bodies of nitrogen after a dive. Diving day after day certainly increases the nitrogen load in our bodies and makes us more vulnerable to decompression sickness. It pays to be extra cautious during multi-day diving. Taking a day off in the middle of a week of diving has been suggested as a precaution.

4.   Do not engage in strenuous exercise after diving. This may precipitate a case of the bends.

5.   Don't be tempted to do something you wouldn't ordinarily do just because you are where it is available. Cave diving, deep diving, interior wreck diving, etc., are all more hazardous forms of diving. All divers need special training to safely participate in these types of activities. Do not be tempted to go beyond your own personal limits. Therein lies danger.

6.   As you may know, divers are likely to get decompression sickness if they fly too soon after diving. DAN advises: wait 12 hours after diving; wait 24 hours after multi-day diving; wait more than 24

New friends swapping dive tales.

hours if you make a required decompression stop dive. You would not want to become ill with decompression sickness on the plane or after arriving back home merely because you made that last dive too soon before your flight.

We all enjoy ourselves when we realize that "island time" is one of the delights of foreign travel. Allowing for minor delays and refusing to let small hassles disturb us will enhance the pleasure of a trip.

Chapter Ten

Dealing with Sexism

"What are you girls doing down here? Diving?
Well, I took a little girl diving once and she
couldn't even get a scallop off a rock."

- Diver encountered on a California beach

In 1968, U.S. Divers, a diving equipment manufacturer, used "It's A Man's World" as their advertising slogan! Thankfully, in recent times things have become easier for female divers. One thing hasn't changed much, though, even in this day and age – sexism in diving. It still runs rampant in advertising, photojournalism, magazines, training, clubs, travel, etc. Women are used as attention getters, used inappropriately in advertising, and are the subject of numerous double-meaning headlines.

Even though women have comprised more than 25% of the diving population for at least ten years, it seems most of the people who write, photograph, and buy space with scuba customers in mind still assume all divers are male.

The entire sporting goods industry has geared up for women. Women represent the fastest growing segment of this consumer group, and manufacturers are responding with gear for women. This is good news for runners as shoe makers are finally producing shoes that fit the female foot. Although some progressive manufacturers of diving equipment are beginning to make equipment designed for women, some have attempted to meet the female divers needs with pastel colors and decollete wetsuits.

Although BC's have become available in fashionably feminine stripe packages, most sizes still remain too large (too wide or too long) for many women. The color of the fabric changed but the basic pattern from which it is cut did not. Although some fins now come in pale blue and pink, the sizes are still the same old medium and large. All manufacturers must realize that an item of equipment is not designed for the female simply because it comes in a color associated with femininity.

Since the vast majority of sports are sold as family-oriented activities, gearing ads to the single male doesn't seem too clever on the part of the diving industry. Women make up a very large percentage of new divers (currently estimated at between 33 and 50 percent) and manufacturers who address themselves to the real needs of these women divers, a large segment of the diving public, will certainly reap the rewards of increased sales.

Women divers must be very aware of potential sexism while purchasing diving equipment. An accomplished female diver recently went into a dive store to purchase a regulator. She had done her research on regulators and had concluded that she wanted to purchase one of the top-rated regulators in the latest U.S. Navy study. The owner of the dive store tried to dissuade her. He told her that she did not need all those features. Its adjustable parts would only confuse and confound

Support the diving manufacturers who have responded to the growing number of female divers by supplying equipment in appropriate sizes.

Women are ready, willing and able to shoulder their fair share of diving responsibilities.

her, and no one at her "level" needed such sophisticated equipment. (He never inquired what her "level" was, however.)

We are amazed at the number of women who arrive at the dive site with soft fins in vibrant colors. The sales personnel seldom seem to take into consideration that women also need powerful fins just as men do. After all, women perform the same dives as men. Salespeople don't spell out the disadvantages of soft fins, especially to their female customers. Although it may be the consumer's responsibility to ask for more information before purchasing, most new divers must buy their basic equipment prior to their first pool session – that is with little or no experience or knowledge of the product. This obviously does not make for informed consumers.

Dive stores should expend more effort to inform new divers or future divers of the advantages, disadvantages and ramifications of the equipment they are purchasing. They should provide this information equally to both male and female customers. This would eliminate the needless replacement of unsuitable or inappropriate equipment within the first year of diving which is common to women divers who were not properly informed when making their initial purchase.

The dive store will retain a good customer for years if they treat women intelligently and honestly from the beginning. Divers must remember the saying "let the buyer beware". New divers, especially female divers, must be on guard and learn to ask the right questions, without being intimidated by sales personnel who may not know as much as you think they do. They may in some cases actually know less than you do.

While in training, be on your guard for double standards. Some instructors find it simpler to assist their female students with "those heavy tanks," rather than instructing her in a tank properly sized for her. Also, watch for preferential treatment – receiving more time and attention than your fellow classmates and receiving more physical affection than your male counterparts. We are not talking here of the conscientious instructor willing to legitimately expend extra effort on a student's behalf but the unscrupulous instructor taking advantage of a female student.

Women make great dive buddies.

Suspect any dive instructor, male or female, who asks to date a student during the course. Even if you refuse the invitation, you cannot be assured of fair and impartial treatment during the course. A conflict of interest cannot be avoided. Ask to be transferred to another class or ask for a refund and perhaps you should contact the certifying agency. All certifying agencies want to be informed of an ethics violation, and trading C-cards for sex clearly falls into that category. Even if the behavior is not so blatant and clear cut, be sensitive to the sexual innuendo.

Some of life's best moments can be underwater.

On the other hand, there are some instructors who give less attention to women because they feel that females won't dive after class is over anyway. It is often difficult to get one of these instructors to take your diving ambitions seriously. It's not unheard of to find an instructor who assumes all women are in class to meet men, or one who assumes a woman will never dive after her class is completed.

Be aware of any instructor who cuts corners for you. You will be the loser. Being towed back to the boat or the beach during your class by that male instructor who feels you just can't perform or make it on your own will not give you the skills to become competent and certified. A quality instructor will help you develop the skills and strength to handle the open water without assistance. It is vital for you to know you can handle the open water situation.

Be leery of any dive leader who disparages you for being apprehensive. Women are usually better than men about owning up to their fears. This is a positive advantage in diving. Be sure to keep in touch with your feelings during training, and feel free to vocalize any concerns. Try to express your concerns clearly and specifically. Your fears should be addressed by the dive leader in a calm, reasonable and non-judgmental way. If your instructor or divemaster belittles you for your apprehensions, find someone else with whom to train and/or dive. You are in much better psychological shape for diving when you are in touch with yourself and know your limitations.

Women are filling leadership roles in the diving industry.

*Take your diving seriously and refuse to be
categorized as a helpless, dependent diver.*

Keep the following in mind:

- You do not have to carry as much equipment at one time as a man.
- You do not have to kick as fast as a man.
- You will enjoy diving even more when you personally participate in your choice of activities (hunting, photography, wreck diving, etc.), but you need do none of these things to be an excellent diver.
- You do not have to walk as fast as a man with your equipment. You can stop to rest. You may make as many trips as necessary.
- You can stay down longer on a tank of air without feeling guilty.
- You can call a dive when you are apprehensive.
- You can lead the dive without threatening anyone's ego.
- You can safely admit you are cold.
- You can actively participate in the dive plan.

- You do not have to merely follow your hunter, photographer, wreck diver, etc., buddy around.
- You can demand your fair share of down time doing the things you like to do, whatever they may be.
- You are certainly free to experiment and dive with different people.
- It is dangerous to be a dependent diver – dangerous for both of the buddies. (It is the follower, not the leader, who is usually left without assistance in time of need.)
- Don't insist that he be the one who always sets the compass course. It is a simple matter to learn underwater compass navigation.
- Don't let anyone else do your dive tables for you. It's *your* life. Both buddies should do the tables independently, in case one has made an error. If you've forgotten how to do them, it only takes a small refresher to relearn. They are easier to do than it seems.
- Don't share a dive computer. A dive computer can only record one diver's profile and you cannot dive exactly the same profile as your buddy. Slight depth and/or time differences can be hazardous.

Women comprise a large percentage of the diving public.

We recently found ourselves diving with a delightful stranger, an instructor. He told us he had so much fun diving with women. For him, women on any type of dive trip always meant a better day.

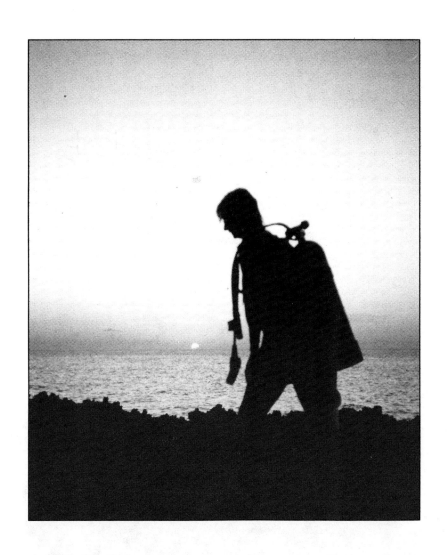

CHAPTER ELEVEN

In Conclusion

"Thank you for giving me the gift of 'the ocean.'
My greatest fear in life has now become my obsession."

Kristina Bork
Los Angeles, California

There is no other sport that so enables us to enter an entirely new world and there is no other sport than demands so much of us. Tennis, basketball, volleyball, mountain biking, running, racquetball, swimming, skiing – yes, these require certain levels of physical fitness but they do not require the ability to determine conditions, analyze time and depth limitations, consider our particular feminine anatomy and physiology and stay in the best shape possible as does scuba diving.

Advanced classes increase knowledge and ability in various areas.

You owe it to yourself to be the best diver you can be. You have already invested a great deal of time, money and effort in becoming a diver. How much more could be required? It depends entirely on how far you want to go.

Be the best diver you can be.

Constantly strive to improve your skills; nothing will bring you more confidence. Take additional classes in the areas of interest to you. Learn rescue techniques; they apply to yourself as well as your buddy. If you have never snorkeled or dived in the ocean, plan a trip with some friends. If you have never visited the lakes or springs, do so and learn about fresh-water diving. Learn about the organisms you visit on your dives. Life underwater is infinitely fascinating. Do you enjoy photography? Underwater photography is one of diving's perpetual challenges — one which will keep you enthralled for the rest of your life.

As diving instructors we utilize every opportunity to learn – workshops, lectures, formal classes or just sharing information and ideas with other instructors. We recommend you do the same.

There are so many experiences awaiting you.

Diving has a tremendous capacity to change your life in very important ways. Women who did not consider themselves physically gifted are ecstatic to find that they are nimble and graceful in the water. The mastery of a sport which so many of the general public regard as impossible will bolster your courage and elevate your view of yourself – uplift your self esteem. This improvement in self-image carries over into all aspects of our life. Your family and friends regard you differently. The assignments you assume at work and in your daily life seem different. Many tasks are made plausible because you know what you have accomplished in the ocean.

*There are many diving activities that provide
fun as well as continuing education.*

Many women combine their love for diving and the sea with their occupations. Writers and photographers specialize in underwater work. Biologists concentrate on life in the oceans. Teachers turn to instructing in diving, oceanography, or perhaps conducting tide pool tours. Divemasters learn to crew and captain diving vessels. There are many jobs in the travel field; many more in the sales field. Retail sales training is a natural forerunner for the successful operation of a dive store. There are varied positions in the commercial diving fields — diver medics, inspectors, welders. While many women have long running, distinguished careers in dive-related fields, there is always room for more in this rapidly growing arena.

When women dive, they bring special talents to a special environment, thereby enriching both themselves and their setting. Women have always been known for social graces, gentle spirit, and the gift for civilizing any situation. It's wonderful we have brought our special attributes to enrich the world of diving.

APPENDIX

CERTIFYING AGENCIES

IDEA
International Diving Educators Association
P.O. Box 17374
Jacksonville, FL
(904) 744-5554

L.A. Co.
Los Angeles County Underwater Program
419 East 192nd Street
Carson, CA 90746
(213) 327-5311

MDEA
Multinational Diving Educators Association
P.O. Box 3433
Marathon Shores, FL 33052
(305) 743-6188

NAUI
National Association of Underwater Instructors
4650 Arrow Highway
Montclair, CA 91763
(714) 621-5801

NASDS
National Association of Scuba Diving Schools
P.O. Box 17067
Long Beach, CA 90807
(213) 595-5361

PADI
Professional Association of Diving Instructors
1243 East Warner Avenue
Santa Ana, CA 92505
(714) 540-7234

PDIC
Professional Association of Diving Instructors
P.O. Box 3633
Scranton, PA 18505
(717) 342-1480 or 342-9434

SSI
Scuba Schools International
2619 Canton Court
Fort Collins, CO 80525
(303) 482-0883

YMCA
Young Mens Christian Association
YMCA National Scuba Program
6083-A Oakbrook Parkway
Norcross, CA 30093
(404) 662-5172

REFERENCES

1. Griffiths, T. Sport Scuba Diving in Depth. Princeton: Princeton Book Co., 1985.
2. Hong, S.K. "Breath Holding Diving Patterns in Ama: Male vs. Female." In Women in Diving: Proceedings of the Thirty Fifth Undersea and Hyperbaric Medical Society Workshop, 1987. Publ. No. 71. Bethesda: Undersea and Hyperbaric Medical Society, 1987, pp. 24-34.
3. Pendergast, D.R., Kame, Jr., V.D., Nawrocki, D.M. "Influence of Fin Selection on Underwater Swimming Performance." Undersea Biomedical Research 18 Suppl. (1991): 67.
4. Mekjavic, I.B. "An Evaluation of Six Fin Designs." Undercurrent 13, No. 9 (1988): 11,12.
5. "An Evaluation of Five Fins." Undercurrent 16, No. 10 (1991): 10-12.
6. Fife, W. Ed. Women in Diving: Proceedings of the Thirty Fifth Undersea and Hyperbaric Medical Society Workshop, 1987. Publ. No. 71. Bethesda: Undersea and Hyperbaric Medical Society, 1987.
7. Bassett, B.E. "Decompression Sickness in Female Students Exposed to Altitude During Physiological Training." Annual Scientific Meeting of the Aerospace Medical Association (1973): pp. 241-242.
8. Bassett, B.E. "Medical Profile of the Woman Scuba Diver." In Proceedings of the Tenth International Conference on Underwater Education, 1978. Colton: National Association of Underwater Instructors, 1978, pp. 41-48.
9. Bangasser, S. "Medical Profile of the Woman Scuba Diver." In Proceedings of the Tenth International Conference on Underwater Education, 1978. Colton: National Association of Underwater Instructors, 1978, pp. 31-40.
10. Zwingelberg, K.M., Knight, M.A., and Biles, J.B. "Decompression Sickness in Women Divers." Journal of the Undersea and Hyperbaric Medical Society, July, 1987.

11. Taylor, M.E. "Women and Diving." In Bove, A.A. and Davis, J.C. (eds.): Diving Medicine, 2nd ed. Philadelphia: W.B. Saunders Company, 1990.

12. Spencer, M. "Decompression Limits for Compressed Air Determined by Ultrasonically Detected Blood Bubbles." Journal of Applied Physiology 40, No. 2 (1976), pp. 229-235.

13. U.S. Navy Diving Manual, Vol. 1. Rev. 1. Air Diving. Washington: U.S. Government Printing Office, 1985.

14. Sleeper, J.B., and Bangasser, S. Women Underwater. Crestline: Deepstar Publishing, 1979.

15. Woodruff, J.J. "What Every Girl Should Know About Diving." Skin Diver, March, 1972, pp. 38, 39, 76.

16. Bolton, M.E. "Scuba Diving and Fetal Well Being: A Survey of 208 Women." Undersea Biomedical Research 7 (1980): 183-189.

17. Gilman, S.C., Greene, K.M., Bradley, M.E., and Biersner, R.J. "Fetal Development: Effects of Simulated Diving and Hyperbaric Oxygen Treatment." Undersea Biomedical Research 9 (1982): 297-304.

18. Bolton, M.E., and Alamo, A.L. "Lack of Teratogenic Effects of Air at High Ambient Pressure in Rats." Teratology 24 (1981): 181-185.

19. Bolton-Klug, M.E., Lehner, C.E., Lanphier, E.H., and Rankin, J.H.G. "Lack of Harmful Effects from Simulated Dives in Pregnant Sheep." American Journal of Obstetrics and Gynecology 146 (1983): 48-51.

20. Lanphier, E.H. "Pregnancy in Diving." In Women in Diving: Proceedings of the Thirty Fifth Undersea and Hyperbaric Medical Society Workshop, 1987. Publ. No. 71. Bethesda: Undersea and Hyperbaric Medical Society, 1987, pp. 3-23.

21. Dunford, R.G., Wachholz, C., Fabus, S., Huggins, C., Mitchell, P. and Bennett, P.B. "Doppler Analysis of Sport Diver Profiles." Undersea Biomedical Research 18 Suppl. (1991): 62.

22. Stone, Dr. T. "Women and Diving." Discover Diving, September, 1991, pp. 44, 45.

23. Dembert, L., and Keith, J.F. "Evaluating the Potential Pediatric Scuba Diver." The American Journal of Diseases in Children 140 (1986): 1135-1141.

24. Davis, J.C. Ed. Medical Examination of Sport Scuba Divers, 2nd Ed. Texas: Medical Seminars, Inc. 1986.